CISTERCIAN FATHERS SERIES: NUMBER TWENTY-EIGHT

STEPHEN OF LEXINGTON

LETTERS FROM IRELAND
1228–1229

ULSTER

Macosquin

Grey
Comer
Inch

Assaroe

Newry

Boyle

CONNACHT

Abbeylara   Mellifont

Abbey Shrule

Knockmoy

Kilbeggan   St Mary's Dublin

Monasterevan

Baltinglass

Corcomroe

Abbeyleix   LEINSTER

Kilcooly

Owney   Killeny   Duiske

Holy Cross

Monasteranenagh   Jerpoint

Hore   Dunbrody

Abbeydorney   Inishlouaght   Tintern Minor

Fermoy

MUNSTER

Middleton

Tracton

Maure   Scale of Miles

0   10   20   30   40   50

CISTERCIAN FATHERS SERIES: NUMBER TWENTY-EIGHT

STEPHEN OF LEXINGTON

LETTERS FROM IRELAND

1228 - 1229

Translated, with an introduction,
by
BARRY W. O'DWYER

Cistercian Publications Inc
Kalamazoo, Michigan
1982

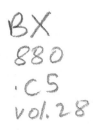

A translation of *Registrum Epistolarum Stephani de Lexinton abbatis de Stanlegia et de Savigniaco*, edidit Dr. P. Bruno Griesser, O.Cist., *Analecta Sacri Ordinis Cisterciensis* 2 (1946) 1–118.

Library of Congress Cataloguing in Publication Data:

Lexinton, Stephen de, ca. 1193–1260.
　　Letters from Ireland, 1228–1229.

　　(Cistercian Fathers series ; no. 28)
　　"Translation of Registrum epistolarum Stephani de Lexinton, Abbatis de Stanlegia et Savigniaco, edidit Dr. P. Bruno Griesser, O.Cist., Analecta Sacri Ordinis Cisterciensis 2, (1946) 1–118"—T.p. verso.
　　1. Lexinton, Stephen de, ca. 1193–1260.
2. Catholic Church—Clergy—Correspondence.
3. Clergy—England—Correspondence.
4. Cistercians—Ireland—History—Sources.
I. O'Dwyer, B. W.　II. Griesser, Bruno.
III. Title.　IV. Series.
BX4705.L6173A4 1982　271'.12'024　81-10116
ISBN 0-87907-428-0　　　AACR2

Typeset by Gale Akins, Kalamazoo
Printed in the United States of America

TABLE OF CONTENTS

Table of Abbreviations vii

I. Introduction 3

II. The Letters 15

The Mellifont Filiation 227

The Cistercian Monasteries in Ireland 228

The Itinerary of Abbot Stephen in Ireland in 1228 . . 229

TABLE OF ABBREVIATIONS

ASOC   *Analecta Sacri Ordinis Cisterciensis*   •

Registrum   B. Griesser, ed., 'Registrum Epistolarum Abbatis Stephani de Lexinton', *ASOC* 2 (1946) pp. 1–118.

Gwynn and Hadcock   A. Gwynn and R.N. Hadcock, *Medieval Religious Houses: Ireland* (London, 1970).

Janauschek   P.L. Janauschek, *Originum Cisterciensium Tomus 1* (Vienna, 1877)

RB   *Regula monachorum sancti Benedicti;* Rule of St Benedict.

Statuta, 1, 2   J. Canivez, ed., *Statuta Capitulorum Generalium Ordinis Cisterciensis,* vol. I, 1116–1220; Vol. II, 1221–1261 (Louvain, 1933–4).

Biblical citations:

Ac	Acts	Jn	John	Pr	Proverbs
Co	Corinthians	Jon	Jonah	Ps	Psalms
Dt	Deuteronomy	1 K	1 Kings	Qo	Ecclesiastes
Eph	Ephesians	Lk	Luke	Tm	Timothy
Gen	Genesis	1 M	1 Maccabees	Ws	Wisdom
Is	Isaiah	Mt	Matthew	Si	Ecclesiasticus
Jb	Job	P	Peter		

Scripture is cited according to the nomenclature and enumeration of *The Jerusalem Bible.*

STEPHEN OF LEXINGTON

LETTERS FROM IRELAND
1228–1229

1

INTRODUCTION

THE REGISTER OF THE LETTERS of Abbot Stephen of Lexington has been published in two parts,[1] of which the first part[2] contains the letters written when Stephen of Lexington was Abbot of Stanley in England in 1228 and 1229 and Visitor of the Cistercian monasteries in Ireland in 1228, before he was elected Abbot of Savigny on 24 May 1229. His notary during his visitation of the Irish monasteries in 1228 and in the period following it, when he had returned to Stanley, was a monk of Stanley. Everything he wrote is related to and is contemporary with matters concerning Abbot Stephen until July 1229, when he left Stanley for Savigny. Everything else in the manuscript is of a later date when Abbot Stephen was Abbot of Savigny. This notary wrote the first three gatherings completely and he began the fourth and the sixth gatherings, which were completed by other hands at later dates. The present order of gatherings in the manuscript is erroneous and, as this order has been followed in the published edition of the Register, the same errors have been reproduced there. The correct order should be: the second gathering, the third, the sixth, the first, and the fourth; this corrected order has been followed in this translation. All the contemporary records of Abbot Stephen of Stanley, which are very largely records of this visitation of the Irish monasteries in 1228, are in these five gatherings; matters relating to the Irish monasteries did continue to come up at a later date, when Stephen was Abbot of Savigny, and have been included with the records of the visitation of 1228 in the published edition,[3] but they are part of the Register kept when Stephen was Abbot of Savigny and are not included in this translation.

Stephen of Lexington was the youngest of four sons of

3

Richard of Lexinton, baron, who took this designation from the manor and parish of Lexington, now Laxton, in the English county of Nottingham. Stephen and his brothers achieved high office in the Church and the law. Robert, Stephen's oldest brother, was an ecclesiastic and a prebendary of the collegiate church of Southwell; he succeeded to the barony of his father and greatly increased the land holdings in the family, and he had a distinguished career as a royal judge. The second boy, John, succeeded his older brother to the family estate in 1250. He was a clerk of the chancery, and distinguished himself in the royal service. For several brief periods he was the keeper (or perhaps the temporary guardian) of the Great Seal. He was Chief Justice of the Forests north of Trent and governor of royal castles in 1255, when he died without issue, in 1257, the family estate passed to the third brother, Henry. Henry was bishop of Lincoln (1254–8) and died the following year, the same year as Stephen, the youngest of the four brothers.[4]

Stephen was graduated Bachelor of Arts from Paris in the first decade of the thirteenth century. After a period of time, probably in 1215, he returned in the normal academic progress to take up the study of theology; for this he returned to his own country, to Oxford. He was presented by the Crown to a prebend in the church of Southwell in 1215, and perhaps his entry as a clerk into the royal service in the manner of his brothers seemed inevitable. But in the course of a lecture given by his master, St Edmund Rich of Abingdon (afterwards Archbishop of Canterbury), at Oxford in 1221, the Cistercian abbot of Quarr on the Isle of Wight entered the lecture hall, and on the completion of the lecture Stephen and six of his fellow students asked the abbot to admit them to the Cistercian Order.[5]

Stephen entered Quarr, and two years later, in 1223, he was made Abbot of the English monastery of Stanley in Wiltshire, a daughter-house of Quarr and a member of the filiation of Savigny. Stanley was the mother-house of the important Anglo-Norman monastery of Duiske in Ireland, founded in 1204. As Abbot of Stanley, Stephen attended the General Chapter in 1227. At which the General Chapter renewed the commission to the abbot of Clairvaux to provide for the visitation of the Irish monasteries. On the recommendation of the abbot of Trois Fontaines, the Visitor in 1227, the abbot of Clairvaux delegated Abbot Stephen. The commission, stated in somewhat more restricted terms than Abbot Stephen had hoped for,[6] was renewed by the General Chapter of 1228, when it was understood that Abbot Stephen would continue to serve as the abbot of Clairvaux's delegate in Ireland.

The product of a distinguished family and of distinguished universities, Stephen took with him to the cloister the predispositions of his upbringing and his station in life. Coming from an able legal family and formed in the demanding intellectual milieu of the universities of Paris and Oxford when the impact of the new Aristotle was beginning to be widely felt, he feared disorder and was ill at ease with ignorance.[7] He looked to education and the institutions of government to restrain the excesses of violence and passion. Rich in intellectual qualities, he also possessed qualities of the spirit; an exemplary monk and a dedicated abbot, he was also a man of genuine holiness who esteemed the rich vein of sanctity which graced the Cistercian Order from its foundation, and he looked for its augmentation in his own day.

In Ireland, he found violence and war in place of an ordered society; instead of the calm and peace of the cloister, he found disorder and irregular observance. It was difficult to predict in the activities of one day what would occur in the days to come. There seemed to be an absence of established norms of conduct, an abandonment of principles of behaviour accepted elsewhere, and a lack of honesty and good faith. His dismay necessarily coloured the policy he adopted towards the Irish monasteries. He did not approach the Irish situation as a problem of souls, but as a problem of regulations, of standards and roles, of rules to be applied and observed.

The Ireland to which Abbot Stephen went in 1228 was in the aftermath and final stages of the Anglo-Norman conquest and settlement which had begun in 1169, Ireland, England, and many other countries formed part of a great cultural and political empire ruled by French knights and French clergy. Different lords ruled this great spread of territory, but those who administered it, both in the Church and for the crown, spoke the same language and were united by cultural ties. The Anglo-Normans in Ireland were composed of various peoples from England, Wales, and the mainland of France, but they spoke the French language and shared in French culture; the kings of England who became Lords of Ireland were Frenchmen. In Ireland in the early decades of the thirteenth century, two different and antagonistic cultures and societies, the French and the native Irish, had remained side by side in a condition of competition and potential conflict with one another as the one strove to survive and the other strove to dominate and transform native institutions and customs.[8]

By the time Abbot Stephen went to Ireland, there were ten French-speaking Anglo-Norman Cistercian monasteries (including a separate group of four Ulster monasteries), and one Welsh-speaking monastery (Tracton). There were twenty-one native Irish monasteries; these formed the filiation of Mellifont, whose foundation in 1142 had preceded the Anglo-Norman conquest. Ten of the Mellifont monasteries were already founded in Ireland by the conquest. In the first half of the thirteenth century the Anglo-Normans held most of the eastern part of Ireland, practically the whole of Meath, including the present-day Westmeath, all Ulster east of Bann and Loch Neagh, and the great plain of Munster.[9] This was the 'land of peace', but at the end of the twelfth century only four or five Cistercian monasteries were situated in areas at peace. Outside this were the 'marches' where a constant struggle was taking place between the two races, and beyond this was the land of the Irish, the 'land of war'. Areas which by 1250 were part of the 'land of peace' were still being actively disputed as 'march' lands when Abbot Stephen was in Ireland in 1228; he described Mellifont as lying in such an area.[10] But even in some pacified areas it took some three generations before the immigrant settlement had reached a sufficient density to bring about a social transformation.[11]

Abbot Stephen began his journey to Ireland very early in 1228; he went first to the monastery of Margam in Wales[12] where he was joined by the abbot of Margam as his companion and fellow-visitor of the Cistercian monasteries in Ireland. Abbot Stephen had originally intended that the other abbot would stay in Ireland until the end of June, but he remained with Abbot Stephen until the end of the visitation in November. Abbot Stephen requested royal protection on his journey before leaving Stanley,[13] and King Henry III had written to the Justiciar of Ireland on 27 January 1228 commanding that this protection be given.[14] Abbot Stephen finally reached Ireland during the month of March. He seems to have disembarked in either Wexford or Waterford, and would have found his first accommodation in either the monastery of Tintern Minor or of Dunbrody.[15]

He spent a couple of weeks in the area of these two monasteries, and his first extant letter seems to have been written from Dunbrody. This letter was addressed to the community of Glanewydan,[16] a small monastery situated near the coast south of Waterford harbour. In it Abbot Stephen indicated to the community that he intended to visit their monastery. No subsequent reference to this visitation is to be found in his letters, but he was in possession of precise information about the affairs of this monastery and this would have come from his own visitation, which would have occurred before he left Dunbrody to set out for Tracton. Towards the end of March or at the beginning of April, he probably took ship from Waterford, or perhaps Wexford, to travel to Tracton, in county Cork. Abbot Stephen does not give any description of his visit to Tracton, but references to it in his letters make it certain that he did visit the monastery at this time. Abbot Stephen could also at this time have visited the monastery of Chore, situated on the north of Cork harbour, with Tracton on the south, but he gave this task to the abbot of Tracton.[17] Abbot Stephen then set out northwards, to journey to the monastery of Maigue, county Limerick. His route should have taken him in the vicinity of Fermoy, and when he was in the vicinity of this monastery he would most likely have called in, and even have stayed a night; but there is no reference in his letters to any contact. The countryside in the vicinity of Maigue was heavily forested and the journey very dangerous for the visitors; he and his party were attacked once or twice and threatened often by gangs of robbers. It is not certain whether Abbot Stephen had intended to carry out his official visitation of Maigue at this time or only to make contact, but in the event his reception in the monastery left him with no choice, for he was attacked within the monastery itself[18] by a group of Irish monks who opposed him and also the Anglo-Norman abbot who had been placed in control of them the previous year. Abbot Stephen's stay at Maigue on this occasion was consequently brief. He then set out for Holy Cross, to reach which he would have travelled first to the monastery of Owney where he would in any case have wanted to discuss the affairs of Holy Cross and other matters with the abbot of Owney. Abbot Stephen's intention was to suppress Holy Cross and to add its lands to Owney, in accordance with the decree of the General Chapter of 1227;[19] he would also have wanted to discuss matters relating to the monastery of Suir with the abbot of Owney, especially as he had decided to suppress Glanewydan, its daughter-house. The abbot of Owney had represented the abbot of Furness as visitor of Suir in the previous year, and Abbot Stephen would also have gone to him for the further information which he set out in a letter to the community of Suir, probably sent from Holy Cross.[20]

Abbot Stephen reached Holy Cross in May; before he left Tracton, he had sent a letter to the abbot of Holy Cross informing him that he proposed to be at his monastery on May 9,[21] and Abbot Stephen clearly intended to spend some time at this monastery looking into its affairs. He left Holy Cross to travel to Kilcooly. In a forest near the monastery, he and his party were attacked by a gang of robbers,[22]

8

and the monks barely escaped with their lives. The attack could have occurred either before Abbot Stephen reached Kilcooly or after he had departed from the monastery for Jerpoint. The visit to Jerpoint on this occasion was only a brief one, paid as it were in passing, but it was sufficient to indicate to Abbot Stephen that at a later time he would need to revisit Jerpoint and make a thorough enquiry into the state of monastic affairs there. On this first visit to Jerpoint Abbot Stephen was met with insubordination, for he was compelled to dismiss the precentor and send him for punishment to the monastery of Fountains in England (the mother-house).[23] One matter which had brought Abbot Stephen to Jerpoint at this time was to do with Killenny; this small monastery had been suppressed by the visitor in 1227, and its lands and property had been united to Duiske. Abbot Stephen would need to take up this matter with Jerpoint, the former mother-house; he would also need to visit Killenny, now under sentence of suppression; the matter also involved Duiske, of which he, as Abbot of Stanley, was also father-abbot.

He probably visited Killenny on his journey from Jerpoint to Duiske, and he intended on reaching Duiske to stay some time there. He had first decided to remain until the end of June to hold a meeting of the abbots of the Cistercian monasteries in Ireland;[24] but he changed his mind later and decided to call the meeting for June 25, at St Mary's Abbey, Dublin. He very probably visited Baltinglass on the way, for the road to the central-south from Dublin passes down the valley and by the monastery of Baltinglass.[25]

Abbot Stephen was in Dublin for the meeting of abbots he had called,[26] and he remained there for another month, until July 26. He had numerous important matters to attend to, among the more weighty of which were arrangements for the elections of new abbots at Abbeyleix, Baltinglass, and Monasterevin; he had decided not to undertake a visitation of Monasterevin despite the bad condition of that monastery and its lack of an abbot, instead having a delegate act for him on that visitation[27] as well as at Baltinglass and Abbeyleix.

He also wrote several letters directed to the General Chapter at Cîteaux, in which he set out the state of things at that time as he saw it in the monasteries in Ireland.[28] He made a quick trip to Mullingar on July 20 to discuss with the Anglo-Norman bishop of Meath, Ralph Petit, certain matters relevant to the monastery of Bective,[29] and returned to Dublin. With this business completed, he prepared to carry out a thorough visitation of Mellifont, a task now made more urgent by the recent resignation by the abbot of that monastery.[30]

Abbot Stephen reached Mellifont on Thursday, July 27, early in the morning. He spent a week in the monastery, leaving it on August 2, having been forced by the state of the monastery to remain longer than he had originally intended.[31] While at Mellifont he wrote to the bishop of Ossory explaining this delay, which had caused a postponement of a planned meeting of the two men and others at Kilkenny; as a consequence of this change of plans, Abbot Stephen then informed the bishop, he intended to be in Kilkenny for their meeting on August 12.[32] On leaving Mellifont on August 2, Abbot Stephen went straight to the monastery of Bective, where he stayed briefly before returning to Dublin, whence he planned to set out on a tour of the monasteries in the province of Munster after first meeting the bishop of Ossory at Kilkenny.

It seems most likely that on leaving Kilkenny after his meeting on the 12th, Abbot Stephen went straight to Jerpoint. He was at that monastery on August 16,[33] and as the preceding day was the Feast of the Assumption it seems certain he would have been in that monastery for the celebration of the feast. He spent a good deal of time in the vicinity of Duiske and Jerpoint at this time, and he put together the major part of the list of injunctions which are entered in the Register under the title of the Visitation of 1228.[34] Abbot Stephen wrote to Suir from Jerpoint and received a reply asking him to delay his visitation; he wrote again saying that he would visit the monastery in the week following August 24.[35]

He had made an appointment to meet the abbot of Owney in the town of Clonmel (about two miles from Suir) on August 26, a Saturday,[36] and Abbot Stephen and his party were there on that day. The abbots decided in Clonmel to send ahead of them a lay-brother and two boy-servants to announce the visitation, but because of the reception they received the visitation did not proceed on that day. Abbot Stephen went to Suir on the following day, Sunday, and he remained in the monastery for three days.[37] He supervised the election of a monk of Furness as Abbot of Suir, and then he departed for Dublin where he had to supervise the election of a new abbot at St Mary's Abbey, Dublin. It is not clear how long he was in Dublin on this occasion, but winter was approaching while he was there[38] and he had also arranged to return to Suir to carry out a visitation of the monastery on September 29.[39] There is no further reference in his letters to this visitation but it is to be presumed that Abbot Stephen was back at Suir at the end of September, as he intended. It was also around this time that Abbot Stephen carried out his previously delayed visitation of Kilcooly.[40] All that remained in the Munster circuit were Fermoy, Abbeymahon, and Odorney, and Maigue and Owney in county Limerick. There is no reference in the Register to any visitation of Corcomroe, county Clare, and Abbot Stephen does not seem to have approached that county at all.

After the visitation of Suir, Abbot Stephen would have returned to Clonmel and it would seem that he then went on to Fermoy. He continued then with the visitation of the remaining monasteries in Munster, and he was in a remote part of Munster, some three days' travel beyond Maigue,[41] when he received news that Irish monks there, acting on a rumour that he was about to leave the country, had rebelled. Abbot Stephen hastened back to Maigue, and he re-entered the monastery after control had been regained. Winter was now at hand and the visitation tour was brought to an official close in November at the Tintern Minor.[42] It is clear from his letters that he had not visited all the Cistercian monasteries in Ireland; his major concern was for the

11

monasteries in the province of Munster. North of Dublin he had visited only Bective and Mellifont, and had had no dealings with the monasteries in the province of Ulster, having delegated his authority as visitor of Newry, Cumber, and Grey Abbey to the abbot of Inch in the same area.[43] The abbot of Shrule and the prior of Bective represented him as visitor at Boyle and Knockmoy[44] in the province of Connacht, which was still ruled by Irish Kings. The official visitations at Shrule, Duiske, Kilbeggan, Abbeyleix, Abbeylara, Monasterevin, and Baltinglass were conducted by the abbot of Buildwas[45] and that at Chore by the abbot of Tracton.

Abbot Stephen left Ireland early in November 1228 to return to Stanley; he intended to return to Ireland in June of the following year to take up again the task of visitation,[46] but his election as Abbot of Savigny brought an end to that plan, and he never returned. The visitation had increased Abbot Stephen's stature in the Order and enhanced his reputation. He was elected Abbot of Savigny on 24 May 1229 and he nominated the abbots of Duiske and St Mary's, Dublin, to carry on the visitation of 1229 in his place, and complete the reform along the lines he had set out.[47]

As Abbot of Savigny, Abbot Stephen undertook a journey to Rome in 1241, to attend a General Council called by Pope Gregory IX, which had as a major purpose the condemnation of the Emperor Frederick II, and it seems probable that his Register went astray by misadventure when he was on ship from Genoa to Rome. Abbot Stephen was in the company of Cistercian abbots and other ecclesiastical dignitaries when the fleet carrying them was attacked by a Pisan fleet in alliance with Frederick II. His brother John accompanied him on this journey as the proctor of King Henry III to the Council, and he may have been responsible for Abbot Stephen's escape from the battle at sea between the islands of Giglio and Monte Christo. In the midst of all the confusion, Abbot Stephen's Register seems to have gone astray, and later found its way to the royal library of Turin.[48] The abbots of Cîteaux, Clairvaux and

L'Epau, who were on other ships in the fleet, were captured and imprisoned at Pisa.[49] The rigours of imprisonment hastened the death of Abbot William of Clairvaux; he died after his release while he was still in Italy. In 1243 Abbot Stephen was elected to succeed him as Abbot of Clairvaux.

Abbot Stephen's years as Abbot of Clairvaux were disturbed by a polemic among senior abbots over the place of higher studies within the Order, and in particular over the setting up of a Cistercian house of studies in Paris. The Cistercian College of St Bernard in Paris was Abbot Stephen's creation. He has used a Paris property of the monastery of Clairvaux to develop a *Studium* which was authorised by a bull of Pope Innocent IV in 1245;[50] the College of St Bernard was acknowledged by a further bull of the same pope in 1254. This issue was finally to bring about Abbot Stephen's resignation and deposition from the abbacy of Clairvaux.[51] Opposition to the policy of instituting higher studies in the Order, which the College of St Bernard represented, was very strong, and led Abbot Stephen in 1256 into conflict with the abbot of Cîteaux and the General Chapter, which deposed him. Pope Alexander IV, in conflict with the General Chapter and the abbot of Cîteaux, demanded the setting aside of the deposition order, or Abbot Stephen's reinstatement. The issue became still more involved when King Louis IX of France intervened, apparently in support of the General Chapter. Abbot Stephen resigned as Abbot of Clairvaux in that year, and died not long afterwards, between May and September 1258.

---

1.   B. Griesser, ed., 'Registrum Epistolarum Abbatis Stephani de Lexinton', *ASOC* 2 (1946) pp. 1-118, 8 (1952) pp. 181-378.

2.   *ASOC* (1946) pp. 1-118.

3.   *Registrum,* pp. 111-6.

4.   For a sketch by W. Hunt of the members of the Lexington (Lexton) family, see *Dictionary of National Biography,* edd. L. Stephen and S. Lee (Oxford University Press, 1963-64 reprint) 11:1081-83.

5.   C.H. Lawrence, 'Stephen of Lexington and Cistercian University Studies in *The Journal of Ecclesiastical History* II (1960) p. 167.

6.   An tAthair Colmcille, *Comhcheilg na Mainistreach Moire* (Dublin, 1968) p. 141.

7.   See B.W. O'Dwyer, 'The Impact of the Native Irish on the Cistercians in the Thirteenth Century' in *Journal of Religious History* 3 (1967) pp. 287-301.

8. See B.W. O'Dwyer, 'The Crisis in the Cistercian Monasteries in Ireland in The Early Thirteenth Century: *Analecta Cisterciensia* 31 (1975) 267-304; 32 (1975) 3-112.

9. For the nature and extent of the Anglo-Norman settlement of Ireland, see A.J. Otway-Ruthven, *A History of Medieval Ireland* (London, 1968) pp. 35-101.

10. Letter 24.

11. The racial pattern of all the rural areas must include the inter-penetration of the native Irish everywhere: see Otway-Ruthven, p. 125.

12. Letter 3.

13. Letter 12.

14. *Patent Rolls of the Reign of Henry III, A.D. 1225-1232* (London, 1903), p. 176.

15. For Abbot Stephen's itinerary, the routes taken and the monasteries visited, see Colmcille, pp. 69-129, and map.

16. Letter 1.

17. Letter 4.

18. Letter 21.

19. Letter 5.

20. Letter 6.

21. Letter 5.

22. Letter 21.

23. Letter 13.

24. Letter 18.

25. Abbot Stephen referred to this location of the monastery and to the continuous traffic past it of members of the Order: Letter 98.

26. Letter 22.

27. Letter 39.

28. Letters 21-26.

29. Letter 47.

30. Letter 27.

31. Letter 27.

32. Letter 53.

33. Letter 65.

34. Letter 50. The claim that this was a visitation of Duiske (G. Mac Niocaill, *Na Manaigh Liatha in Eirinn 1142-c. 1600* [Dublin, 1959] p. 143) has been refuted by Colmcille, pp. 131-32.

35. Letters 61, 62.

36. Letter 63.

37. Letter 88.

38. Letter 59.

39. Letter 66.

40. Letter 71.

41. Letter 89.

42. Letter 78. A more accurate text, adding the names of four abbots and this place of meeting, is in Harleian MS Charter 75, A.5, referred to in W. de Gray Birch, *History of Margam Abbey* (London, 1897) pp. 221-22, and printed in G.T. Clark, ed., *Cartae et alia Munimenta quae ad Dominium de Galmorgancia Pertinent* (Cardiff, 1910) No. 855.

43. Letter 51.

44. Letter 55.

45. Letter 56.

46. Letter 94.

47. Letter 98.

48. *Registrum*, p. 3.

49. See *Registrum*, p. 7.

50. See L. Lekai, *The Cistercians: Ideals and Reality* (Kent, Ohio, 1977) p. 82.

51. This controversy has been described by Lawrence, pp. 169-78.

THE LETTERS

I

TO THE COMMUNITY OF GLANEWYDAN,[2] greetings. On the coming to this region on the authenticity of the General Chapter with full powers of undertaking and making provision for the reformation of the Order through the whole of Ireland, we have received reports that certain monks have ill-advisedly and imprudently dispersed and squandered the possessions of your house. We very strictly command you by virtue of obedience as devout sons in Christ of obedience and the Order to show diligent and effective concern for everything, both lands and other properties, which are your responsibility, not allowing any monk of your house or of any other house to cause dispersion of this type by sale, encroachment, or alienation of any kind whatever in future, so that God and the Order ought worthily to commend you for your obedience. We are prepared, when the opportunity presents itself, to make provision for your house with the counsel of worthy men and also yours in accordance with what we consider to be most pleasing and acceptable to God, the Order, and you. Farewell.

---

1. *Registrum,* No. XI.
2. Glanewydan (Vallis Caritatis, Glangragh) in the diocese of Lismore, county Waterford, a daughter-house of Suir: Gwynn and Hadcock, p. 133.

2 [1]

T O THE ABBOT OF WHITLAND,[2] greetings.

Having taken your position into account and also the need there is for your counsel and presence in your own house, we do not advise or dare to advise you to undertake such an arduous and lengthy journey from your own house as the journey to Ireland lest jealous people may perhaps say what we recall is written about the Exodus: Imprudent is he who, having abandoned his own dead, weeps for the stranger. On that account, we undoubtedly indicate to Your Beloved that, the Lord willing, with the counsel of worthy and God-fearing men and having God and the rules of the Order before our eyes, we will devote ourselves to the visitation of your daughter-house,[3] making provision for it as for all the other monasteries in Ireland in accordance with what the discipline of the Order and deeply-rooted discretion on weighty advice directs and obliges us. Farewell.

---

1.   *Registrum*, No. XII.
2.   Whitland (Albalanda, Alba Domus) in the diocese of St David's, Carmarthenshire, Wales, a daughter-house of Clairvaux: Janauschek, 61.
3.   Tracton (Albus Tractus), in the diocese of Cork, county Cork, founded from Whitland in 1225: Gwynn and Hadcock, p. 143.

3 [1]

TO THE ABBOT OF RIEVAULX, greetings.

We acknowledge with great trust in the Lord the fervour of religion and the strict implementation of our way of life, and we commend the lord abbot of Margam[2] for his proven zealousness in respect of our Order; for we considered that we particularly needed the association and the maturity of the counsel of this man in the laborious and difficult Irish matter, especially as he had been a well-informed and useful companion of the visitors in the preceding year, above all in those things which concern this aforesaid matter of the Order. Consequently, after we departed from you and while we were at Roche Abbey,[3] we repeatedly required of him by letter and through the lord abbots of Tintern[4] and Vaudey,[5] and furthermore we ordered him with the authority committed to us, to put every excuse aside out of regard for the reputation and the perpetual honor of the Order, and to take up the aforesaid task with us with the greater willingness the more it was sure to be more dangerous and greater in merits than any other.

Finally, having taken into consideration that he might not give sufficient importance to the force of the command, we went personally to the monastery of Margam, and having publicly stated our authority there in the hearing of all in chapter, we strictly enjoined on him by virtue of the obedience which is owing to the lord abbots of Cîteaux and Clairvaux and to the General Chapter not to attempt to avoid so rewarding and so necessary an obedience. At first he was reluctant to agree, but having deliberated on and carefully considered our admonition in the company of the fourteen monks of the special council of his house, he did not then dare to oppose such salutary admonitions and the commands of his superiors.

On which account, we appeal with all the fondness we can to our claim on your love—on which, as you well know, we especially rely—that you postpone the visitation of the house of Margam in all respects until after the octave of St John the Baptist. For, the Lord willing, the abbot of Margam will have returned from Ireland by that time[6] and you will be sure to find him there. This will allow you to carry out corrections with greater freedom and more fruitfully, if there is anything in that house which needs to be corrected. In addition to this, the presence of the aforesaid lord abbot and the depth of prudent counsel in the visitation and restoration of the monastery of Whitland is now almost reduced to nothing, to use an expression; those very things are of the utmost importance to you, indeed beyond all else we are aware of. In the meantime, you can very carefully and profitably carry out your visitation of and negotiations with the Order in Scotland, concerning which we had discussions with one another. Further, if it pleases you, take down carefully and clearly the letter to our beloved in Christ, Brother Garth, monk of Clairvaux, knowing that we retain the copy of this with us, so that we know what such a reasonable request to so beloved a man can achieve in so worthy a cause. Farewell.

---

1.   *Registrum,* No. XIII.
2.   Margam in the diocese of Llandaff, Glamorganshire, Wales, a daughter-house of Clairvaux: Janauschek, 107.
3.   Roche Abbey (Rupes) in the diocese of York, England, a daughter-house of Newminster: Janauschek, 95.
4.   Tintern in the diocese of Hereford in Monmouthshire, Wales, a daughter-house of L'Aumone: Janauschek, 19.
5.   Vaudey (Vallis Dei) in the diocese of Lincoln, England, a daughter-house of Fountains: Janauschek, 94.
6.   Abbot Stephen had intended that the abbot of Margam would return to his monastery by the end of June 1228.

4 [1]

To the community of chore,[2] greetings.

The charge of much disorder as well as rebellion and conspiracy—which we mention not without sorrow—perpetrated in your house in the past year against the visitor sent to you on behalf of the General Chapter, namely the abbot of Tintern Minor,[3] has been brought to our attention by reliable and trustworthy men. He removed your former abbot, Brother R., from office for refusing to submit to the authority given to him, and at the same time he placed your church and you yourselves under interdict and suspended you from the divine services for as long as you supported the before-mentioned R. as abbot or recognized him as your abbot.

Therefore, with great bitterness of heart at such disobedience and rash presumption against your mother, the Cistercian way of life, which has borne you in Christ, and pondering moreover on such a clear and abominable danger to souls before God and men in that, despite being under interdict and suspended from the ecclesiastical offices, you have still attempted to celebrate these until now, we have delayed quite a long time so that we would do what ought to be done in such a difficult case where such offences have taken place. However, desiring now to spare your ignorance and thoughtlessness in so far as we can and ought, and to provide for the salvation of your souls, we have sent the lord abbot of Tracton and two monks to you, and with the authority given to us by the Chapter and the Order we have given them the faculty of granting absolution in the form we have prescribed to them to all penitents in your house who are prepared to give worthy satisfaction to God and the Order, and of punishing all who are rebellious and disobedient to the above-stated authority, in accordance with justice.

Furthermore, we have bestowed on them the authority of being able to grant dispensation in the case of devout and worthy penitents from the penances deservedly imposed on them previously, and they will exercise their powers during the divine services in due time and place.

Therefore, as beloved sons of God and of obedience in Christ, being mindful in your heart of hearts of how many and how enormous were the remembered offences, although you have been transgressors, hasten now to return to your heart, picture to yourselves the horrors of hell and the glories of heaven in the eyes of your mind, and thus having more perfectly repented in this way, you will be much more sincerely prepared to submit to whatever is necessary for the sake of avoiding the death of the soul than to whatever you underwent for avoiding the death of the body, so that in this way, to whatever extent your contumacious disobedience has scandalized the Church of God and the Order, so to that extent will your devout and humble repentance in Christ cause edification and rejoicing. Farewell.

---

1.   *Registrum,* No. XIV
2.   Chore (Chorus S. Benedicti, Monasterore, Midleton) in the diocese of Cloyne, county Cork, a daughter-house of Maigue.
3.   Tintern Minor (De Voto, Tinterna Parva), in the diocese of Ferns, county Wexford, a daughter-house of Tintern: Gwynn and Hadcock, pp. 142-43.

5 [1]

TO THE ABBOT AND COMMUNITY OF HOLY CROSS,[2] greetings.

The Lord willing, we will come to your house on the Tuesday immediately after the Ascension,[3] carefully to examine your lands and possessions on the following day, and, with the advice of prudent men, to deliberate in accordance with what was decreed in the General Chapter as to whether your house can continue as a monastery on its own or whether it should be joined with Owney.[4] Therefore, we order your abbot by virtue of obedience, which he owes to the General Chapter and under penalty of deposition, to be present and to provide a suitable place for us and the other abbots who are coming there, and also other necessities for us and for our horses. He should also see to it that all the possessions of the house are clearly and distinctly written down on a parchment, what utensils, clothes, cows, bullocks, sheep, books, and all other possessions there are, and what men he has, monks and lay-brothers or seculars, who know the lands and properties of the house and will give us a full and honest account of them, so that with this information having been carefully gathered beforehand we can proceed in a sensible and prudent manner to deliberate on and decide what should be done in regard to your house. Keep this letter until our arrival and return it to us so that we will know how you have responded to our mandate in this regard. Farewell.

1. *Registrum*, No. XV.
2. Holy Cross (Sancta Crux) in the archdiocese of Cashel, county Tipperary, a daughter-house of Maigue: Gwynn and Hadcock, p. 134.
3. 9 May 1228.
4. *Statuta*, 2:62.

6 [1]

TO THE COMMUNITY OF SUIR,[2] greetings.

In your prudence we trust you are aware of the manner in which the General Chapter properly came to dispose of certain monasteries of this province, and on its authority conferred your house on the monastery of Furness as a perpetual daughter-house,[3] acting on the settled conviction that with the help of God the reformation of the Order would be promoted from there. Therefore, as the before-mentioned Chapter transmitted its authority to us with full powers over everything which concerns that aforesaid matter, we strictly enjoin upon each and every one of you by virtue of the obedience which is owing to the General Chapter and the Order, putting aside all opposition, kindly to give obedience with all devotion and humility as sons of the Church and the Order to the monastery of Furness[4] as mother-house in future, and to the lord abbot of that house as father-abbot, receiving with all meekness and reverence the lord abbot of Owney and Brother R., monk of Furness, to whom your spiritual father, the abbot of Furness, has committed his powers if he cannot come himself, and kindly give your consent to them and to their fruitful admonitions as to men deserving of respect who are sent to you with the paternal authority.

Having God before our eyes, we ourselves, together with your father-abbot if he comes, or the aforesaid men if he happens to be absent, will give devout consideration in a time and place available to us to the reforming of the observance and to the appointing of an abbot in your house in accordance with the mandate of the General Chapter.[5] In addition, by this letter of ours with the authority of the General Chapter and the Order we transfer to the house of

24

Furness the full possession of whatsoever rights and powers are known to obtain in relation to a daughter-house according to the rules of our Order. In witness of which matter etc. Farewell.

---

1.   *Registrum,* No. XVI.
2.   Suir (Inishlounaght) in the diocese of Lismore, county Tipperary, a daughter-house of Maigue: Gwynn and Hadcock, p. 135.
3.   *Statuta,* 2:62.
4.   Furness in the diocese of York, England, a daughter-house of Savigny: Janauschek, 97.
5.   The visitation of Suir and the appointment of an abbot there were postponed to the end of August: Letter 62.

7[1]

T O THE ABBOT OF FOUNTAINS,[2] greetings.
On the advice of worthy men we have absolved and completely reconciled Malachy, formerly abbot of Baltinglass[3] and the bearer of this letter, to the Order, as he has often devoutly sought forgiveness and mercy from us with all humility. We transfer him to your house on condition that he remain there for a considerable period because we consider it right for a spiritual father to send his spiritual son on pilgrimage to a distant land until such time as he returns to the father with sincere contrition, having wept with greater abundance and with better intentions in the presence of others. As regards the censure and discipline of the Order, subject the aforesaid monk when he comes to you to the penalty for conspirators until you receive other instructions from the General Chapter or from us. Farewell.

---

1.   *Registrum,* No. XVII.
2.   Fountains in the diocese of York, England, a daughter-house of Clairvaux: Janauschek, 37.
3.   Baltinglass (Vallis Salutis) in the diocese of Leighlin, county Wicklow, a daughter-house of Mellifont: Gwynn and Hadcock, p. 127. In the General Chapter of 1227, Baltinglass was made subject to Fountains: *Statuta,* 2:62.

8 [1]

TO THE ABBOT OF FOUNTAINS, greetings.
Having in mind the great paterfamilias who restored with kindly ease the returning and penitent son to his first place, and also the precept of our master by which he taught that mercy in judgement must always be exalted above all else,[2] on the advice of reliable and God-fearing men we grant as a pardon that when Your Holiness has observed the penitential practices and devout humility of Brother M., formerly abbot of Baltinglass, with the authority of the General Chapter and the Order you can gradually release him by dispensation after the [Feast of the] Exaltation of the Holy Cross[3] from the punishment for conspirators for which he was placed in your house, so that he is fully absolved from the aforesaid sentence by the feast of St Denis[4] unless some new fault, may it never happen, is committed, in which event he would not deserve to enjoy such a pardon. We also grant that he remain with you from the before-stated feast of the Holy Cross for a period of two years, and then if he has behaved well and wished to, he is to be given permission on the completion of the two years to return freely as required to the Irish region. Farewell.

For Brendan, subprior of Jerpoint,[5] a similar letter to the same abbot.

---

1. *Registrum*, No. XVIII.
2. RB 64:10.
3. 14 September 1228.
4. 9 October 1228.
5. Jerpoint in the diocese of Ossory, county Kilkenny, a daughter-house of Baltinglass: Gwynn and Hadcock, p. 136. In the General Chapter of 1227, Jerpoint was made subject to Fountains: *Statuta*, 2:62.

9[1]

T O THE ABBOT OF MARGAM, greetings.

On the advice of worthy men we transfer to your house as to the maternal breast, Brother Patrick, formerly subprior of Maigue,[2] who has devoutly sought forgiveness and mercy from us for his offences. Show a fatherly face of compassion with great mercifulness and kindness to him in the sight of God and the Order lest he be overwhelmed by excessive grief. However, as regards the censure of the way of life[3] and the discipline of the Order, subject him when he comes to you to the penalty for conspirators until you receive other instructions from the General Chapter or from us. Farewell.

---

1.   *Registrum,* No. XIX.
2.   Maigue (Nenay, Monasteranenagh), in the diocese of Limerick, county Limerick, a daughter-house of Mellifont (Gwynn and Hadcock, p. 141), was made subject to Margam by the General Chapter of 1227: *Statuta,* 2:62.
3.   *religio.*

IO [1]

TO ALL THE FAITHFUL OF CHRIST, greeting in the Lord.

It is permitted to our beloved brothers Isaac and Jacob, formerly monks of Holy Cross, and Flan, lay-brother of the same house, to devote themselves to the solitary and eremetical life which they have ardently longed to do for a long time, but they did not attempt to free themselves to fulfil this desire because they knew full well that it is not permitted to monks of the Cistercian Order to do so without the agreement of the General Chapter. Hearing that the authority of the before-mentioned Chapter with full powers throughout Ireland was given to us, they supplicated with all the force they were capable of through themselves and through reliable and God-fearing men that they be permitted by us to turn to the fulfilment of their intention.

Therefore, having deliberated with devout and prudent men and having carefully considered their advice, we graciously consent to the petitions of the aforesaid monks and lay-brother, absolving them from their obedience to the Order, that they may strive to follow the eremetical life with complete religious devotion from now on. In addition, we fully subject the three mentioned men to the jurisdiction of the archbishops or bishops in whose diocese they take their vows, so that, should they learn that through the persuasion of the devil they deviate from the requirements of their holy calling into a scandal to religion, they will remove our habit from them and will punish them in whatever ways they consider to be most beneficial for the salvation of their souls and the honor of the Church and the Order. In witness of which matter etc.

1.   *Registrum,* No. XX.

II[1]

To the abbot of Dunbrody,[2] greetings.

As full powers have been given to us to do whatever we consider to be most advantageous for the salvation of souls and for the honor of the Order with respect to all the monasteries of Ireland and the persons who are there, with that aforesaid authority we strictly enjoin Brother D., your lay-brother, by virtue of obedience to make a year's stay with the abbot of Holy Cross so as to assist him and restore the house which is now almost ruined. On this account in order that the merit of obedience cannot in the passage of time fall to the detriment of the aforesaid lay-brother, who properly should be considered deserving of praise before God and man, we kindly beg Your Holiness out of your boundless generosity to grant this to him by your will and pleasure. Further, if necessary, by virtue of the obedience which is owing to the Order and the General Chapter, we strictly admonish you to receive him kindly at whatever time he returns to you or to your house, and to show fatherly care to him with so much the greater kindness in that he has never attempted, in obedience to the command of the Order and the General Chapter, rashly to withdraw himself from very great dangers and labors. Farewell.

---

1.   *Registrum,* No. XXI.
2.   Dunbrody (Portus St Mariae) in the diocese of Ferns, county Wexford, a daughter-house of St Mary's Abbey, Dublin: Gwynn and Hadcock, p. 131.

12 [1]

TO THE ABBOT OF TINTERN MINOR, greetings.
Our friend Master P. of Christchurch has notified us that although because of the urgent needs of your house you had bestowed certain land in Munster on him by mutual agreement for the term of his life by annual installments, and you transferred possession of the same land to him by your letter, but you have delayed so far despite your promise and to his cost to confer your charter in regard to this. Consequently, since he does not have the proviso of the charter, [that land] is left vacant and unused. Therefore, out of love of justice and the unity of our Order and desiring your advantage and honor according to God, we admonish you with all the affection we are capable of, acting on behalf of our beloved and special friend, to allow that which was properly agreed to between you, as we have asserted above, to be observed in the proper manner, especially as an action which a religious congregation of the faithful has decided to contract with a prelate after careful consideration should not be cancelled with loss of reputation to either party; for you ought to realize that it is of little advantage to you to withhold the charter from him while Master P. has entrance to the possession of the aforesaid land by the authority of your letter, which clearly contains the terms of the transaction, and to that extent he is in possession. But, as of now, you should act in such a way in regard to this matter so that he is not obliged to take action henceforth for what is lacking and so that our special friend will dispose himself to favorable actions to our Order and us. Farewell.

---

1. *Registrum,* No. XXII.

13[1]

T O THE ABBOT OF FOUNTAINS, greetings.

With the authority of the Order and the General Chapter and on the advice of worthy men, we transfer C., formerly precentor of Jerpoint, the bearer of this letter, to your house, commanding you to receive him when he comes to you and to show mercy and kindness to him in so far as you can according to God and the Order. But as regards the censure of religion and the discipline of the Order, subject him when he is with you to the penalty due to slight faults for three days, suspend him from the service of the altar until the Exaltation of the Holy Cross,[2] and put him in the lowest place until released by the General Chapter or by us, yet he may still celebrate the divine services after the afore-mentioned term has been completed, if you are assured of his humility and penitence. Farewell.

---

1.   *Registrum,* No. XXIII.
2.   14 September 1228.

14 [1]

To the abbot of Buildwas,[2] greetings.

By neither pen nor tongue am I able to express the extent of the sorrows and anxieties with which we are afflicted in these days. Daily we are delivered into the hands of our mortal enemies and we feel the whole day threatened with death like a sheep for the slaughter. Therefore, desiring to discuss these and other matters of this kind with you so we might receive consolation through you, we would look forward eagerly to your arrival with us, were it not that having been very shaken by the wind of fear, always on the move, never stable,[3] we scarcely have the power to know in the evening where we will be on the following morning. We are so burdened with so many anxieties and threatened with such dangers, that we beseech you to remember us in your prayers. We have passed on what we cannot include in this brief letter to the bearer to report to you in person. Trust him, if it please you, as you would us. Farewell.

---

1.   *Registrum,* No. XXIV.
2.   Buildwas, in the diocese of Chester, England, a daughter-house of Savigny, was mother-house of St Mary's Abbey, Dublin: Gwynn and Hadcock, p. 130. The abbot of Buildwas was a companion of Abbot Stephen on the visitation, and was then probably in Dublin.
3.   Cf. RB 1:11.

15[1]

TO THE ABBOT OF FURNESS,[2] greetings.

If we endure labors and sorrows and indeed dangers every day without any interruption for you and for all others who have been allotted daughter-houses in Ireland, you would think, we undoubtedly believe, that we deserve your complete sympathy and that you would show greater care and diligence concerning the house entrusted to you; for in your interest and for our own peace of mind, we deliver ourselves every day into the hands of our mortal enemies for your glory, laboring and spreading the seed of the Lord, but you have entered into our labors and freely reap and receive what we sow. For this reason, we hoped you would see that we were well supplied in provisions and in numbers of persons for the assistance for your house,[3] as was enjoined on you by the General Chapter and as you promised us in your letter, and also that you would apply yourself, in respect of your devotion for one another which is still just beginning, to develop this into greater reverence and finally into love by the performance of good works.

Therefore, as we have deferred to you so far in all things which concern the present matter in so far as we can in accordance with the Lord, and are still prepared to defer to you, we bring ourselves with all the insistence we are capable of to request, admonish, and advise Your Paternity, for the sake of God and in respect of the Order, keeping in mind the responsibility enjoined upon you by the General Chapter and agreed to by you with us, to make adequate provision for your aforesaid daughter-house both in temporalities and in spiritualities in accordance with what is enjoined upon you, as stated in these binding letters. For while we are of the view that you come before the rest in this regard, still the

34

lord abbot of Margam comes before you all, and many others should follow his example, for even when his house was sorely harassed by enemies in his region, he not only exposed all his own concerns out of regard for the present matter but also gave himself up to danger by coming with us into Ireland, and he ordered his adopted daughter-house in accordance with our judgement and provided abundantly for it in people and in other ways. Therefore, as you hold a position in no way inferior to his, we beseech you humbly and devoutly in the Lord Jesus, advising and warning and, if necessary, enjoining upon you by the authority of General Chapter, that being at least stimulated by his example, you engage yourself to supply in future an abundance of those things for the advancement of your daughter-house for which up till now you have provided almost nothing, so that God will deservedly reward you and the General Chapter will bestow very abundant thanksgiving on you, and we will not have good cause to complain about you.

You should not be surprised that we did not apply ourselves to expel the Irish,[4] as some considered we would do, because this would be completely against your interests and that of the Order. For it is necessary that we eradicate them little by little and by stages lest perchance the beasts of the field increase in number against us; by beasts of the field I mean these bestial men who, having increased in number in the open in the fields and mountains, would drive away and destroy everything without distinction in revenge for their people. But we have passed on that which we cannot include in the brevity of a letter to the bearer of this letter, Brother A., monk of Fountains, to report to you in person; give complete trust to him in everything, as if to us. Farewell.

Recall to mind that this is already the fourth time we have written to you about this.[5] Therefore we beg you, if you wish to retain your aforesaid daughter-house in your possession, send quickly one of your monks to us, a humble, calm, kindly, wise and discreet man, whom we can make abbot in the aforesaid house, and who knows how to conform to the customs of so fierce a people and to seek the support of Lord Richard de Burgh, the Justiciar of Ireland.[6] For we will not prescribe anything else for the aforesaid house until we have received your reply. Therefore, if it please you, do not delay letting us have your reply in order that we can know what to write to the General Chapter in this instance. Know also that, together with a number of abbots and reliable and discreet men, we went to the house of Holy Cross and having made a careful investigation we found that the house has thirty ploughlands and a valuation of some forty and even more; whence, acting on their advice and with the authority of the General Chapter, we decided that it should continue as a monastery and we have appointed an abbot there.

---

1.   *Registrum,* No. XXV.
2.   Furness in Lancashire, England, a daughter-house of Savigny.
3.   Suir, which by the decree of the General Chapter in 1227 was affiliated to Furness, *Statuta,* 2:62.
4.   *Gentes.*
5.   The other three letters to the abbot of Furness are not included in the Register.
6.   Richard de Burgh was appointed Justiciar 13 February 1228: *Handbook of British Chronology,* p. 148.

16[1]

T O THE ABBOT OF FOUNTAINS, greetings.
    If we endure labors and sorrows etc. as in the preceding letter down to through the performance of good works.[2] But the bearer of this letter and his servants have asserted in our presence that they received nothing from you apart from what was scarcely sufficient for the journey. Therefore, being rather surprised at these and other of their responses, we had thought of restoring the houses entrusted to you to the control of the Chapter, but wishing to respect your integrity, we proceeded to make arrangements for them with the advice of worthy men according to the authority given to us, and with the unanimous election of all the brothers we solemnly appointed one of those whom you sent us from your house as abbot in the house of Jerpoint.

Therefore, as we have deferred to you so far in all things etc. as in the other letter excepting Recall to mind that already.[3]

---

1.   *Registrum,* No. XXVI.
2.   The first paragraph of Letter 15 was included in this letter.
3.   The second and third paragraphs of Letter 15 were included in this letter.

17[1]

TO THE ABBOT OF MELLIFONT, greetings.
If you were to investigate this desire of ours, about which we long to speak with you, you would be moved to admiration to a remarkable extent, seeing the bitterness of our soul and the anxieties we bear. Since we love you in a more special way than the others, it is sweeter than honey and the honey-comb[2] to clear the air and reveal to you what lies hidden in our heart, and it is pleasing that, restored by a mutual exchange of ideas, we would satisfy this anxious longing of ours, even if not wholly then at least in part; since we are not allowed this by distance of place and complete separation of persons, we have tried to express our thoughts within the brevity of a letter, and we pass on whatever is lacking in the present writing to the bearer of this letter, Brother A., monk of Fountains,[3] to report to you in person. Trust him as you would us in those matters which he will report to you on our behalf. Farewell.

---

1. *Registrum,* No. XXVII.
2. Ps 19:10.
3. This monk was also the bearer of Letter 15. Both letters were written at the same time.

18 [1]

T O THE ARCHBISHOP OF CASHEL,[2] greetings, with
a will prepared to pay respects with all reverence and
veneration.

We have received a very carefully composed letter from
the lord abbots of Cîteaux and Clairvaux, in which they
devoutly supplicate, admonish, and command us by the
authority of the Order to render effective assistance in every
way we can through ourselves and our friends to the bearer
of this letter, Brother Vincent, in the matters he has to deal
with for the house of Cîteaux, just as we value the honor of
being Cistercians. Therefore, acceding as we ought to such
exhortations and intercessions, and even more to commands,
we earnestly beg Your Holy Paternity with all the devotion
we can that, having God and your honor in mind, you kindly
receive the aforesaid representative and provide pleasing and
kind assistance to him in the matter entrusted, so that the
lord abbot of Cîteaux and other Cistercian friends who will
hear of this may have your devotion to the house of Cîteaux
and the Order deservedly commended before God and men.

Further, we wish Your Beloved to know that certain
abbots will make a journey to the Chapter within the octave
of Blessed Bernard,[3] and we will be meeting with them in
council on the day of the apostles Peter and Paul[4] at
Duiske;[5] consequently, if you want anything of the matters
which concern you to come to us, you should convey them
safely to us through some discreet person of your household,
and know for certain that Brother Malachy, whom we treated
with such kindness in respect of your petition, has done
nothing at all of what he promised. We have borne with him
so far out of consideration for your honor and reverence;
consequently, if on the prudent and careful advice of

important men we have to take appropriate action against him, Your Paternity should not be surprised or disturbed, for it is necessary; but if we chastise him, we will do so sadly and unwillingly and only because we are compelled by absolute necessity. We would prefer, if we could, to proceed little by little in a spirit of leniency in all our actions; but there are some so stiff-necked and indomitable in heart, who are so determined towards their own destruction, that nothing will put any sense into them save only punishment, and not just any punishment but only that which is austere and hard, which will be with a crook of iron and in a scorching wind.[6] Farewell.

1.   *Registrum,* No. XXVIII.
2.   Marianus O Briain, formerly Bishop of Cork and a Cistercian monk of the monastery of Suir, was provided to the See of Cashel on 20 June 1224; *Handbook of British Chronology,* p. 322.
3.   20 August 1228 was the feast day; the General Chapter was held at Cîteaux around September 14.
4.   29 June 1228.
5.   Duiske (Graiguenamanagh, Vallis S. Salvatoris) in the diocese of Leighlin, county Kilkenny, a daughter-house of Stanley in Wiltshire, England; Abbot Stephen was thus the father-abbot of this monastery: Gwynn and Hadcock, p. 133.
6.   Cf. Ps 2:9, 11:7.

19 ¹

T O THE PRIOR AND COMMUNITY OF BUILDWAS, greetings.

We know that the presence of the pastor and spiritual father is rightly pleasing and welcome to his religious sons, and vice versa. On that account, immediately after Pentecost[2] your abbot most insistently pleaded with us to be allowed to depart from us and return to you. But as we consider that his counsel is essential in the difficult matters and negotiations of our Order, we have arranged with the authority of the General Chapter, even though he is unwilling and resisting, to keep him here with us who are delivered every day—blessed God!—into the hands of our mortal enemies, and where no-one gives us support and consolation save God alone and our company of faithful and spiritual men; since you are rightly obliged by your religious profession to pray continuously for us, so you should pray with the more patience and devotion in so far as we have decided henceforward to increase with grants and build up with honors not only your own house but also its filiation.[3]

Farewell always in the Lord, and know for certain that your aforesaid lord abbot cannot take ship to you for any reason before the feast of St Matthew,[4] for it is necessary that he labor with us in the concerns of our Order and in the midst of continuous mortal dangers. Farewell.

---

1.   *Registrum,* No. XXIX.
2.   14 May 1228.
3.   The filiation *(derivatio)* of Buildwas in Ireland consisted of St Mary's Abbey, Dublin (daughter-house of Buildwas) and Dunbrody and Abbeylara (daughter-houses of St Mary's Abbey, Dublin).
4.   21 September 1228.

20[1]

T O THE ABBOT OF TINTERN, greetings.

We have kept the lord abbot of Buildwas with us in Ireland on the authority of the General Chapter because of the very demanding matters of our Order, which are quite well known to you. Therefore, we have come strictly to admonish and exhort Your Beloved Paternity with the aforesaid authority to engage yourself to carry out devoutly and carefully the visitation of Quarr[2] and Buckfast[3] which have been committed to you by the lord abbot of Buildwas, so that souls may be saved and the zeal for the Order may always be prudently exalted and grow. Take the abbot of Kingswood[4] with you for the purpose of counsel and assistance, or some other devout man whom you decide upon. Take up the aforesaid task with such a spirit of devotion that even though you necessarily have to obey the commands of the Order you will in this at least be participants in our sorrows and merits before God. For we are exposed every day to death and tribulation for the salvation of our brothers and for the laws of our fathers, and we already deservedly reckon ourselves as sheep for the slaughter;[5] blessed be God in all respects, for no-one else gives us consolation and support save Himself alone and the holy and devout prayers of men of good will. Farewell.

---

1.   *Registrum,* No. XXX.
2.   Quarr Abbey in the diocese of Winchester on the Isle of Wight, England, a daughter-house of Savigny, and the mother-house of Stanley: Janauschek, 99.
3.   Buckfast in the diocese of Exeter, England, a daughter-house of Savigny: Janauschek, 103.
4.   Kingswood in the diocese of Gloucester, England, a daughter-house of Tintern: Janauschek, 58.
5.   Acts 8:32.

21 [1]

To the abbot of citeaux and to the community of abbots in General Chapter, greetings.

It is unbecoming for us to detain Your Paternity for long with our letter, for we know how occupied and burdened you are in many ways with unavoidable and demanding concerns of the Order. However, we have decided to bring to the attention of Your Holiness as briefly as we can this particular matter in Ireland, with all that is necessarily connected to it, which was committed to us by your authority, and we entrust the remainder to be faithfully reported by the venerable men who are bearing these letters, through whom you can be more fully instructed about what has been done and at the same time what danger there is in Ireland.

We decided to cross over to the before-stated parts only after having first exchanged opinions about the manner of proceeding with abbots of England and Wales, and also having sought patronage and protection from the lord king[2] and from those bishops and magnates of the kingdom by whom it was considered that a way could be prepared or a passage opened up in this matter. Having dealt with these matters in the usual manner, we came to Ireland where we heard of enormous crimes and horrible and notorious conspiracies which they were shameless enough to add this year to the former offences against those representing our Order; and so first of all we took care with a devout preliminary admonition given in the chapter-house to convince the communities of each monastery we entered to beg humbly for the benefit of absolution. They did this; but we would only grant the aforesaid grace of absolution with the greatest solemnity so that they would abhor similar crimes in future and would be fully aware of the magnitude of their offences, the enormity of which has everywhere scandalized both clergy and people. Therefore, while all rose to their feet in the chapter-house and faced the Book of the Rule placed in a conspicuous position, the whole chapter firmly promised that they would never perpetrate such things in future or give their support to such perpetrators, and so they were absolved in the church before the Eucharist.

We immediately returned to the chapter-house and only then did we begin to take up with them those matters which were incumbent on us in our position. The appeal of modesty and the tediousness of verbosity compel us to say nothing more about the number and the abominable gravity of their crimes, and to keep the knowledge of them away from the hearing of such holy men. But we will conclude with a summation: those things which have been brought to our notice so far by visitors or by others by word of mouth or letter are of a less serious nature than the things we ourselves have reliable evidence of and in part have seen with the witness of our own eyes. For we have with us the seal of a certain abbot which was pawned in a tavern for eighteen pence, and we saw the seal of another abbot in the same manner in the possession of a secular; consequently, on account of this the monasteries are reduced almost to nothing; that which had twenty plough-lands at foundation now, to speak the truth, does not have three; that which had eighty does not have fifteen, and so of the others. Consequently, compelled by need almost all those in charge of the land wander away from the cloister as they please under the pretext of begging; there is no silence, no monastic discipline in the chapter-house, few are living in community, but they live in miserable huts outside the cloister in groups of threes and fours; they take up a collection and send to the village traders to purchase what they need instead of making use of the provisions of their properties. We are ashamed to mention the contagion of the flesh, the association with robbers and murderers, and others of the same ilk; however, this state of things is quite well known through reports of other visitors. Internally all the spiritualities are dissolved, externally the temporalities are almost completely wasted, so that for the most part we can say in truth: there is nothing of the Order there apart from the wearing of the habit.

Therefore, venerable fathers, it is incumbent on you to remove so great a loss of souls and such a cause of shame in our Order with the proper remedies, and know beyond doubt that unless you press on very urgently and vigorously with the already-commenced reformation of our religious life, not sparing expense or even bodily danger, then the Order which has languished for so long a time and now shows only the marks of eternal death will never be restored to life again; on the contrary, if this illness continues unchecked—may it never happen—then it will weaken the Order in every way like a malignant cancer, and we are convinced that it will take possession of other peoples: he who does not take care to apply with perseverance the needed correction in the least important realm even diminishes little by little the respect for the aforesaid Order in the major realms; for the will to sin lives in many people, and the sinful action will follow if no punishment is feared. Dearly beloved fathers, give attention to this for ephemeral and temporary medicine is of little use, though recovery will come from perseverance and diligence.

But we forbear to mention how we escaped mortal dangers from robbers in the wood outside Kilcooly[3] and in the monastery of Maigue and in many other places; indeed, we are delivered every single day into the hands of our mortal enemies, and also our companions who are undertaking with us the duties of the Order, so that already we reckon ourselves rightly as being sheep for the slaughter; but we are prepared devoutly to bear all this with joy and gladness for Christ and the laws of our fathers if we feel that your strengthening hand is with us, and if we know that some fruit will result from this trial, and that we will one day reap with joy from the seeds which, God knows, we are sowing in tears[4] so that in some way we will see the flourishing of our holy Order in our days.

And so, having exchanged counsel everywhere with worthy

and God-fearing men, religious and secular, of high rank and low, we succeeded in discovering one solitary path of recovery and restoration, which we send to Your Holy Paternity under our seal and that of the abbots of Ireland; kindly act in accordance with what is stated there, and confirm it with your authority and insert into the statutes of the present year, lest the enemy, who—blessed be God—has already shown himself for his part to accept the discipline of the Order because of our admonitions and instructions, will entrench himself for ever against us and the visitors sent after us, and we, who were sent to this region with your authority, will be exposed through negligence to mortal danger or perpetual confusion in this regard, to the shame and scandal of our religious life. Farewell.

Do not neglect to ask for further information, if it please you, from the bearers of this letter, and send your wishes to us through them, writing back to those who are in the midst of continual tribulation day and night. On account of this state of things, kindly grant dispensations from coming to the General Chapter this year to the recently-appointed abbots who are indeed learned and devout men. For the pressing urgency of these matters as well as their complete lack of temporal substance excludes all action against them in this regard.

---

1. *Registrum,* No. XXXI.
2. Letters of protection were issued by King Henry III on 27 January 1228 to the Justiciar of Ireland: *Patent Rolls of the Reign of Henry III,* p. 176.
3. Kilcooly (Arvicampus) in the archdiocese of Cashel, county Tipperary, a daughter-house of Jerpoint: Gwynn and Hadcock, p. 137.
4. Cf. Ps 126:6.

22 [1]

COUNCIL OF ABBOTS.
When the venerable man, the abbot of Stanley came to the region of Ireland with the authority of the General Chapter, he undertook to summon us together and very firmly to engage us there under oath on the authority of the same Chapter and the Order to determine carefully how the Order there could recover and be restored to its proper state. Therefore, having taken into consideration all the circumstances of the monasteries and of the persons living in them, and the bestial habits of the same region, and having also pondered on the advantage and benefit of the Order on the one hand, and on the other the wrongs and dangers which modest respect as much as tedious prolixity compel us to pass over in silence, we have been unable to discover any other means of bringing an end to the horrible conspiracies and inveterate disorders, and of reviving religious life, except that some monasteries be taken away from obedience to undisciplined houses and be subjected by perpetual law to monasteries in other realms than their mother-houses, which are ready and able quickly to restore the ruin of the Order in spiritualities and temporalities; each mother-house has at least two-daughter houses in the aforesaid land, so that should one of the two attempt to shake her neck from beneath the yoke of the Rule and the Order with contumacious and evil conspiracies and create detestable schisms, then the mother can at least find refuge and acceptance in at least one daughter-house while she strives to curb the insolence of the second; in this way, in accordance with the differences of conditions or times, she will conveniently and effectually remove the oppression and subdue the pride of the one through the other.

Further, since it is to be feared that the enemy has free entry and reaps the fruits when anyone applies himself unwillingly and slowly to heavy tasks and to expensive and especially to dangerous labors, with the authority of the General Chapter and the Order we have each and all decided to impose perpetual silence in every way on everyone, abbots, monks and lay-brothers, no matter where they are from, so that they are not permitted to protest in any way against the following decree or to make any attempt to interfere with it; moreover, it is decreed that whatever is claimed or attempted to the contrary at any time and in any way whatever is null and void.

Therefore, all the council came to one and only one decision as to what was most necessary for the restoration of Order and the preservation of the same in its proper state, and it was this: that the monastery of Clairvaux should have as daughter-houses the houses of Boyle,[2] Bective,[3] and Knockmoy,[4] together with Mellifont; the monastery of Fountains the houses of Baltinglass, Jerpoint, and Monasterevin;[5] the monastery of Margam the houses of Maigue, Holy Cross, Chore, and Odorney; the monastery of Furness the houses of Owney,[6] Suir, Fermoy,[7] and Corcomroe;[8] the monastery of Buildwas the house of Kilbeggan[9] together with Dublin.[10] Further, because the small monastery of Glanewydan is extremely poor and completely lacking in movable and immovable possessions, and also has a great shortage of personnel, it is to be joined in perpetuity with all its granges and appendages and with all its legal rights to the monastery of Dunbrody, by reason of its proximity and on account of the many advantages which will accrue to the aforesaid house and to the Order; the major reason for this is that in the same small monastery there are no more than eight monks and nine lay-brothers and it does not have three plough-lands of land intact, all of its movable and immovable possessions having been almost completely wasted or wholly alienated.

In addition to other innumerable reasons for a decree of this nature, there is one which should be especially noted, and it is that in this way that pernicious unity which

48

provided the opportunity for the unheard-of conspiracies and disorders in this realm on many occasions will certainly be dissolved. For while scale presses on scale there is never an opening which is left between them.[11] Further, the proud rebellion and the very ferocious threats of Mellifont would never be suppressed while darkness protects darkness itself.[12] Also, the small monastery of Shrule,[13] formerly a daughter-house of Mellifont, which does not have more than five plough-lands of land, is given as a daughter-house to the monastery of Bective, which is in a very strongly fortified position to which the visitors can have safe entry and secure abode so that it will be of great help in assisting its mother, Clairvaux, in subduing and reforming both Mellifont and Boyle. For it is no more than fifteen leagues distant from Mellifont. Therefore, strong in the faith by which we are bound to the Order, we testify that there is no other way more advantageous and more fruitful or as convenient for the restoration to the Order, and indeed it should strive most strenuously for renovation, for as soon as the opportunity is lost it will certainly degenerate into its old ways unless the matter is thoroughly carried through in accordance with the procedure stated above; if any other decision is reached, then it is useless to send visitors in future, whether ourselves or others, unless it be for our death and the perpetual shame of our Order. Also, it is very strictly enjoined upon the father-abbots named above that they, together with the visitor of the General Chapter, strive energetically and effectively for the reformation of their aforesaid daughter-houses immediately after the aforesaid meeting. Further, be it known for certain to all men that unless what the before-mentioned meeting has undertaken in this regard is prosecuted with the greatest constancy, then like a malignant cancer this sickness will also infect other peoples with its pestilential example, and gradually, which may the Most High prevent, it will weaken the authority of the General Chapter and will destroy the reputation of the whole order. In witness of which matter etc.

1.   June 25, from Dublin.
2.   Boyle (Ath-da-Larc) in the diocese of Elphin, county Roscommon, a daughter-house of Mellifont: Gwynn and Hadcock, p. 128.
3.   Bective (Beatitudo Dei) in the diocese of Meath, county Meath, a daughter-house of Mellifont: Gwynn and Hadcock, p. 128.
4.   Knockmoy (Abbeyknockmoy) in the archdiocese of Tuam, county Galway, a daughter-house of Boyle: Gwynn and Hadcock, p. 124.
5.   Monasterevin (Rosea Vallis, Rosglas) in the diocese of Kildare, county Kildare, a daughter-house of Baltinglass: Gwynn and Hadcock, p. 142.
6.   Owney (Abington) in the diocese of Emly, county Limerick, a daughter-house of Furness: Gwynn and Hadcock, p. 126.
7.   Fermoy (Castrum Dei) in the diocese of Cloyne, county Cork, a daughter-house of Suir: Gwynn and Hadcock, p. 132.
8.   Corcomroe (Petra Fertilis) in the diocese of Kilfenora, county Clare, a daughter-house of Suir: Gwynn and Hadcock, p. 130.
9.   Kilbeggan (Benedictio Dei) in the diocese of Meath, county West Meath, a daughter-house of Mellifont: Gwynn and Hadcock, p. 137.
10.   St Mary's Abbey, Dublin (S. Maria iuxta Dublinum), a daughter-house of Buildwas: Gwynn and Hadcock, pp. 130-31.
11.   Cf. Jb 41:7.
12.   Cf. Jb 40:17.
13.   Shrule (Abbeyshrule, Flumen Dei) in the diocese of Meath, county Longford, a daughter-house of Mellifont: Gwynn and Hadcock, pp. 125-26.

23 [1]

TO THE GENERAL CHAPTER. [2]
Venerable Fathers, we have been particularly careful to reach no decision about what ought be done in this aforesaid matter except with authoritative counsel and deep and mature reflection, for safety reigns where counsel abounds. [3] Although, as prudent men would agree, the safer course for us would have been to decide what should be decided and to change what ought to be changed on our departure from the region of Ireland, we have, however, taken into account that it would be dangerous even to the point of death for those remaining after us and we preferred to go ahead ourselves rather than have so great and holy a people perish.

Therefore, having summoned at the monastery of Dublin a meeting of abbots and also priors of those houses to which abbots had not been appointed, and having received the complete approval and agreement of all, we ordained, promulgated, and solemnly required the execution on the day after [the feast of] Blessed John the Baptist of the resolution contained in the charter, [4] to which all appended their marks. Further, we also drew up for each monastery a proper and authentic document with our seal and that of all the abbots affixed, strengthened by perpetual bestowal and confirmation, and we also gave authentic and absolute authorization through the abbots themselves or through persons acting for them with power of attorney. We permitted these abbots, as fathers-abbot, [5] to appoint abbots and make visitations after receiving our instructions. Therefore, we solemnly enacted whatever we could for precautions's sake and complete security so that in consequence the mother-houses would be greatly encouraged in carrying out the reformation of their daughter-houses. For the one and only law of religious

51

life followed by them, although they were wearing the Cistercian habit, was this: whatever is pleasing is permitted. No-one is surprised about the fornication of monks and lay-brothers, for one only wonders about those things which are rarely found, as the philosopher says. Therefore, who will involve themselves with a company of such criminals or expose themselves or theirs to such danger for the reformation of the houses unless in regard to the adopted daughter-houses they are rendered completely certain without any grounds for fear that eventually they will reap those fields with joy which undoubtedly they will sow for many years with tears?[6] It would indeed be a cruel and damnable result if mothers worked and deprived themselves of possessions and people for the reformation of their daughter-houses, and finally strangers introduce their own people without hindrance after some nine or more years of labor and effort. Therefore, reverend fathers, it is appropriate to your authority and our humble ministry to make solemn provision in all possible ways that the before-stated groupings are established in perpetuity, and it pertains to your venerable constancy to support your interest and to consolidate it very firmly in the statutes of the present year in order that our ministry may not be despised, and the venerable reverence for your authority may not perish and come into disrepute, for we have continuously and fervently striven for this with every ounce of discretion and caution, as God is our witness, even up to the point of giving up the ghost.

Further, may I be allowed to speak in full freedom of spirit to our Lords and Fathers, pronouncing and proclaiming this one thing, that it is inappropriate for holiness which is so distinguished and adorned with such mature constancy to treat matters lightly, for just as nothing is taken up unadvisedly, so should that which has been laudably begun be prosecuted with a constant and indefatigable heart to its worthy conclusion. Therefore, we write this to Your Paternity stating the pure and simple truth, having experienced that poetical saying to be very true; 'Less vividly is the mind stirred by what finds entrance through the ears'[7] etc. And so it would have been pleasing to us, and more acceptable and sweeter than honey and honey-comb,[8] had we been allowed to be present in person at your holy congregation,[9] and even more to entreat with the living voice rather than with a dead letter in the presence of such an audience. But our recently appointed abbots held us back and restrained us, although unwilling and resisting, for they feared that after our departure plots would be prepared against them similar to those which were made for the new abbot of Baltinglass after the departure of the lord abbot of Froidmont in the previous year.[10] Therefore, they asserted that if we departed so suddenly they would immediately resign and, following on our departure, would straightaway withdraw. But it is becoming for Your Devoted Reverence to rejoice especially and to glory in the Lord in this, that no-one, whether lettered or lay, secular or religious, made any resistance to the above-stated decree when it was promulgated in the usual manner; on the contrary, everyone, the Irish as well as other peoples, united together in one voice and glorified and praised God, saying that this was done by God alone, who puts down the mighty from his seat and exalts the humble,[11] who resists the proud and gives favor to the meek[12] so that the evil men will learn not to blaspheme in future, nor to walk with erect head against the law of God and the institutes of religious life, but rather they will keep innocence and behold justice, since nothing but this is left for those who have made peace with the Lord their God.[13]

Therefore, all that remains is firmly and vigorously to prosecute that which has been begun, and next year to send discreet and prudent visitors to whom respect will be given and honor shown by all on account of the authority and support they receive from God and from the royal and ecclesiastical power; they will eagerly advance along the pre-ordained way of the King and worthily lay on a solid foundation gold, silver and precious stones, never deviating lest perchance they destroy what has been built, and make this last error worse than the first.[14]

1.   *Registrum,* No. XXXIII.
2.   June 25, from Dublin.
3.   Cf. Pr 11:14.
4.   Letter 22.
5.   The term *pater abbas (patres abbates)* refers to the abbot of the monastery's mother-house, who had visitation rights over the monastery and its abbot. The modern term among Cistercians is 'father immediate'.
6.   Cf. Ps 126:6.
7.   Horatius, *Ars Poetica,* 180: Horace, *Satires, Epistles and Ars Poetica,* ed and trans. H.R. Fairclough (Cambridge, Mass.: Loeb Classical Library, 1955), pp. 464-5.
8.   Ps 19:10.
9.   The meeting of General Chapter at Cîteaux.
10.   Abbot Stephen described what happened on that occasion to the abbot of Trois Fontaines: Letter 28.
11.   Lk 1:52.
12.   Cf. Pr 3:34, Jm 4:6, 1 P 5:5.
13.   Cf. Ps 36:37.
14.   Cf. Mt 12:45.

24 [1]

To the abbot of clairvaux,[2] greetings.
We are unable to write with a pen or fully to express
in words how many labors and sorrows we have borne in
Ireland for the laws of our fathers and out of respectful
obedience to your command, walking over this realm in a
spirit of great desolation with frequent shedding of tears and
sowing the seed of the Lord that somehow the aforesaid
land, so long dry and barren, might receive rain on itself and
might at least grow grass in season from these seeds with
which it is sown, which in time to come will fructify into a
harvest. And may the Father of mercies be blessed in all
respects for, having himself opened his hand, the animals (for
this is a bestial people, I do not say wholly but to a great
extent) are sprinkled with goodness[3] in so far as it is possible
among such rough and hardened material; for the Most High
has rained down his justice a little over them—not that his
virtues have yet rained in abundance, not that the cataract
of heaven has yet opened[4]—but whatever has begun to come
to life through his grace has happened with the wonderful
co-operation of the Lord and by means of great diligence and
cautious discretion. For we have devoted ourselves to acting
at one time with fear, at other times with love, with prayer,
with threats, with blandishments, with harshness; on other
occasions we threatened them very severely, calling heaven
and earth against them—that is, divine chastisement and the
secular power in accordance with the power given to us,
for they must be judged in future as being not just disorderly
people, or even conspirators, but rather as disgraceful
schismatics. Consequently, just as the Church is generally
accustomed to act against heretics or schismatics, so should
proceedings be rightly taken against them by the sons of the

Church, that is, by the Cistercian Order; and this is correct, both clergy and people declare and demand it be so. Those people who think that they can be freed from the office of the spiritual authority never fear to be masters of the errors of those who are subject to them.

Further, while scales adhere to scales there was never an opening which was left between them, and they were indomitable while darkness protected darkness.[5] For while Behemoth as a strong man fully armed, with a multitude and with cunning iniquity mounts guard over his own palace, his goods are left in peace.[6] Therefore, it was necessary for us in the first place to divide his kingdom cautiously so that eventually it can be laid waste. Therefore, we came to the conclusion that daughter-houses should be separated from mother-houses, and daughter-in-law from mother-in-law, to use an expression of the evangelist,[7] that in this way those who formerly belonged to our enemies rather than to us might begin to strive for the Lord. We also decided carefully to assign more daughter-houses to each ordained mother-house so that it could conveniently and in perpetuity freely control the one through the other, and keep subdued in humility that one which raised the head so insolently and disrespectfully in unheard-of pride and abuse.[8] Therefore, the small monastery of Bective and the monasteries of Boyle and Knockmoy were allotted to Your Paternity, and to the house of Clairvaux, the house of Holy Cross together with Maigue to the monastery of Margam, Kilbeggan to the monastery of Buildwas, because it has a very observant daughter, that is, the monastery of St Mary's, Dublin. Two were assigned to the monastery of Fountains in the previous year, that is, Baltinglass and Jerpoint; one to the monastery of Furness, that is, Suir and also that of Owney, which it formerly held. In addition, we have joined and united the small house of Glanewydan, which does not have in all three plough-lands, to the nearby monastery of Dunbrody.

We have ordained nothing concerning Mellifont because the abbot has not come to us, and neither has he sent anyone to us as yet, but we are quite hopeful that it is subdued and fully under control. For they were fearful, seeing that we have the royal power with us as well as the ecclesiastical censure should the matter have to come to the stage of judgement. But we consider it necessary that the lands be exchanged and the monastery transferred, even if the same amount of property acquired by exchange cannot be easily found. For half the land in a safe place and in a land of peace would be better than the whole complement in the area where it now is. For it is in a very bad and dangerous march-land between the English and the Irish. Because of this, though there may be peace by the hour there, there is how-ever no constant peace, no secure peace; and because only punishment wipes off the dust of pride and removes the beam of obstinacy from the eye, it presents itself in future, prompt and subdued to obey our council in all respects. We have left it only two daughter-houses and one grand-daughter-house, and we have threatened to pluck it com-pletely if it attempts at any time to take off on former flights of pride.

Therefore, the experienced diligence of Your Holiness can determine in part with what careful consideration and moderation of counsel our whole program of ordinances has been carried out; we have done nothing improper in this regard, nothing unconsulted, nothing in haste, nothing in arrogance, God knows, but we cannot convey this in dead letters or explain it through someone else's voice. Therefore, prostrate at the feet of Your Paternity, we humbly beg with tears that you not permit either us or yourself whose office we bear, or our mother Clairvaux and all of our filiation, to be exposed to perpetual confusion on account of negligence or faint-heartedness in this matter; may it never happen, but rather, my father, Israel's chariot and charioteer,[9] stand up firmly for your interest because piety praises it, necessity requires it, and the benefit of the Order and the salvation of souls commends it. We are also concerned to some extent about the lord bishop of Cashel who is delaying at Cîteaux;[10] you know him to be a respecter of the nation and not of strict religious life, an acceptor of his people rather than the well-ordered mind of a stranger.

Further, that perverse and wily fox Malachy, formerly abbot of Baltinglass, having received advice and support from some of the Irish, so they say, is making a journey to Cîteaux or to the Roman Curia in order to create disturbance and confusion with his lying stories at a time when there is no-one present to oppose him and to speak the truth about those who are absent. He was excommunicated and publicly denounced by the visitors last year because he refused to return the seal with which he made on the aforesaid house many false claims, which were very much to its detriment. He was absolved by us and reconciled to the Order on account of the most earnest entreaty of the lord archbishop of Cashel, being sent to the house of Fountains on condition that he keep himself under the judgement of the Order, and return the seal and charters of Killenny[11] which had been removed in secret and which he had publicly confessed to have with him, along with many privileges of Baltinglass. He was in a position to do this because he was the harborer of some conspirators and malefactors together with the goods of that house which they had taken in the last of the recently formed conspiracies against the new abbot appointed there by the aforesaid visitors. We transmit his wretched career to Your Holiness, although it is not the full story.

The first, second, third, fourth, fifth day was given to him but he did nothing. For he had not returned to his Lord God with his whole heart but with falsehood, as the result shows. Finally, having been deservedly restored to his former sentence by the council of the abbots of Ireland on the day of Blessed John the Baptist,[12] he was solemnly excommunicated by all at Dublin and was denounced on account of his manifest contumacy and his enormous and great sacrilege, as was previously mentioned; consequently, if it please you, hold this opinion of him and have him denounced in chapter at Cîteaux and Clairvaux so that he does not seduce the simple-minded through his craftiness.[13] In addition, there is need to take precaution and to make careful provision that there is someone to oppose him in Rome, if he reaches there, for we have carried out the whole of this aforesaid matter diligently and devoutly, in the midst of great and continuous mortal danger, not looking to rewards or seeking repayments, keeping in mind that gifts blind the eyes of judgement and bend the strength of authority. When we were at houses or granges we accepted not a cow, not an ass, not a piece of cloth, not a penny, indeed nothing at all apart from food and drink alone. Consequently, Holy Father, it is up to you to provide for our small house over which we preside in one way or another, and from which alone we received sustenance, for neither honor nor any advantage has accrued to it from the allocation, lest we let our labors sink to the depths or by impunity let some stain sully the praise of God and our ministry, of whatever kind it may be.

Kindly study with care and diligence the letter which we send on this matter to the lord abbot of Cîteaux and to the General Chapter and, if it please you, cause it to be read out clearly in the hearing of the Chapter, or of those inquiring into misuses, just as your holy and esteemed prudence will know to be most advantageous. Nor should your sincere and devout humility attribute it to arrogance if for once we speak to our Lord and Father, not presuming to teach but to advise a wise man concerning the way in which the confirmation should be phrased in the statutes, because it would perhaps be tedious to go into the involved reasons for our ordinance. If it please you and you see it to be advantageous, the confirmation could be made quite effective in this manner:

> The ordinations and also the changes concerning the houses of Ireland made for the reformation of the Order by Brother S., Abbot of Stanley, Visitor with full power in the year of grace 1228, are approved and are confirmed in perpetuity with the authority of the General Chapter. In addition, it is decreed that whatever is claimed or attempted to the contrary at any time and in any way whatever is null and void.

Further, we have entrusted whatever the above-stated matter involves and is not included in the present writing to the bearers of this letter, to be very faithfully reported in your pious hearing. We desire our sub-prior, whom we have enjoined to go to you on this matter, to find favor in your eyes. Arrange for him, if it please you, that he can be present in the holy General Chapter to provide information on matters of obscurity and to dissolve doubts if any dispute is stirred up concerning the matter referred to; as for himself, he has labored bravely and fervently at our side throughout Ireland, always near us as a faithful helper and tireless companion. May Your Holiness prevail in the Lord, one with our mother Clairvaux, which I pray will never abandon the ancient paths of our most blessed patron, Most Blessed Bernard, but, as she has done so far, will enkindle herself with the odor of his esteem, both in seasoned love and in the fervent spirit of religious life, and with the cup of spiritual grace will inebriate the whole Order which—oh what a sorrow!—already shows laxity on all sides, or, rather, to put it more clearly, is almost become emptied out, the whole Order having become not just carnal but the flesh itself, not just terrestrial but engrossed in the things of the earth, not Israel but rather Idumea.[14] Therefore, Venerable Father, may the spirit of the Lord and the disposition of Bernard pour into you; for on you in the principal seat there is concentrated such dishonest cupidity, such indecent impurity, such neglicent laxity in regard to religious life, such eager activity in trading, which day by day attacks and dishonors all that is becoming in our Order before God and men. It is on you, I say, who is so pure and distinguished before all other members of our Order that there is no-one through all the ends of the earth who doubts that you should occupy the position of our celebrated patron. May he himself preserve you in holiness and health to the praise and honor of his Order and the grace and glory of his house.

---

1.   *Registrum,* No. XXXIV.
2.   Dublin, around June 25. Radulphus de Roche-Aimon was Abbot of Clairvaux: d'Arbois de Jubainville, *Études sur l'état interieur des abbayes Cisterciennes* (Paris, 1858), p. 179.
3.   Cf. Ps 145:16.
4.   Cf. Gen 7:11, 8:2.

5.   Cf. Jb 41:7, 40:17.
6.   Cf. Jb 40:10, Lk 11:21.
7.   Mt 10:35.
8.   Cf. Ps 30:19.
9.   Cf. 2 K 2:12, 13:14.
10.   Archbishop Marianus O Briain of Cashel had gone to Cîteaux while Abbot Stephen was in the midst of his visitation; he had arrived back in Cashel by the end of August, when Abbot Stepehn wrote to him: Letter 64.
11.   Killenny (Glandy, Vallis Dei) in the diocese of Leighlin, county Kilkenny, a daughter-house of Jerpoint: Gwynn and Hadcock, p. 138. In the General Chapter of 1227 Killenny was suppressed as an independent monastery and united to Duiske: *Statuta,* 2:62.
12.   June 24.
13.   In the General Chapter of 1231 Malachy was described as one whose malice was notorious; in the General Chapter of 1233 he was referred to as the old persecutor and destroyer of the Order, sufficiently well-known for his malice: *Statuta,* 2:95, 124.
14.   Cf. Ezek 35:15.

25 [1]

T O THE PRIOR OF CLAIRVAUX,[2] greetings.

We trust Your Prudence is aware how difficult and in many ways dangerous is the task which your lord abbot imposed on our shoulders, namely the matter of Ireland. For this reason, we have sent to Clairvaux as the bearers of this letter venerable men to whose lips we have entrusted many details to be reported more secretly and at greater length both to the lord abbot and to you and the council. Therefore, be good enough to receive them with kind favor for the sake of God and the Order and for the honor of Clairvaux, and give a favorable hearing to them; if it please you, arrange entry for the aforesaid messengers to the aforesaid lord abbot lest the Irish business be frustrated or destroyed—to the perpetual scandal and the ignominious disgrace of Clairvaux, may it never happen, when because of it we are delivered every day into the hands of our mortal enemies at the command of the lord abbot. It is especially incumbent on your experienced skill to provide the means by which the mouth speaking evil[3] is blocked lest our mother Clairvaux with her whole filiation be ignobly besmirched with a mark of shame through failure or faintheartedness in this regard, and deservedly lie open to the backbiting of rivals, of whom, as you have certainly learned, there is no small number. A house which is so genuine in its religious life and its holiness and so distinguished by its public counsel should take up nothing inadvisedly, inasmuch as it is known to be the foundation, the stimulus, and the model of our entire Order through the merits and instruction of Blessed Bernard, so should that which has been laudably begun be emphatically and firmly prosecuted to its worthy conclusion. Farewell.

1.   *Registrum,* No. XXXV.

2.   July, from Dublin, Gulielmus de Montaigu was Prior of Clairvaux: d'Arbois de Jubainville, *Études,* p. 194.

3.   Cf. Ps 34:10, 1 P 3:10.

26[1]

T O THE ABBOT OF VALLOIRES,[2] greetings.
We have sent venerable men bearing this letter to the
General Chapter on behalf of the Order in Ireland and the
enormous offences which were unheard-of for ages. Therefore, acknowledging special trust in the Lord, we kindly
appeal to your gracious love and devotion for the sake of
God and of compassion for the Order in Ireland, already
languishing in such a way as to show everywhere the marks of
death, to receive the aforesaid men kindly and give them a
favorable hearing, so that being more fully instructed by
them you can stand firm in the Chapter and become as an
unshakeable wall for the sake of the house of the Lord and
the honor of religious life, very much threatened with
destruction; do this much, if it please you, so that God will
reward you as you deserve, and the fervor of our Order, now
grown tepid, will re-kindle with glory and honor, at least for
the future, as the crown of your labor, and will be re-
established in its proper state by means of your devout
concern. Farewell.

---

1. *Registrum,* No. XXXVI.
2. July, from Dublin. Valloires (Valloriae) was in the diocese of Amiens,
France, a daughter-house of Cîteaux: Janauschek, 52.

27 [1]

TO THE ABBOT OF CLAIRVAUX,[2] greetings.
R., formerly Abbot of Mellifont,[3] has come to us
and shown us your letter concerning the acceptance of his
resignation. Having carefully studied this and deliberated on
it, we have finally done what you ordered, Venerable
Father, though regretfully and wishing it had been possible
conveniently to do otherwise, for we considered him to be
essential because of the inviolability of his conscience and
the zeal of his devout affection, as well as the regard which
the English have for him over others of the aforesaid house
of Mellifont. Being very concerned not to bring about his
death through a lack of judgement on our part, we were by
no means prepared to allow him to return to Mellifont. For
certain beasts of savage, not human, mind, in which nothing
or very little follows the ordered movement of reason, were
threatening to murder him not just in secret but even openly
in our hearing and that of many others. However, after the
humble resignation had been made, the aforesaid Brother R.,
like a fearless lion, quite disregarded the danger to his own
life and himself offered to strive with us for the restoration
of the before-mentioned house if we would enjoin this on
him by virtue of obedience and remission of sins. But this
was something we would not attempt to do, and neither
would anyone suggest that we should.

Therefore, having first prepared the way in so far as we
could by prayers and then by preaching and conferences,
and also having threatened them often and seriously and
cropped their horns for the great part by taking away the
daughter-houses, we finally entered Mellifont together with
two abbots and many monks prepared to face death for the
laws of our fathers and the purgation of sins, with the

cross of the Lord as our protection, on the Thursday immediately after the feast of Saint James,[4] before Mass. There,
while they shouted threats from all sides, we waited silently
and in patience to see whether divine condescension would
open his hand and the heavens would rain down from
above[5] and would sprinkle such savage, such unruly spirits
with some benediction. And God be blessed, what we were
waiting for happened suddenly and unhoped-for, for the
divine clemency shone forth wonderfully and mercifully
in a great and prudent concern. For, God is my witness, we
did not cease to harangue this bestial people for seven days
on end, and we were often overcome by such exhaustion that
we could scarcely say a word or open our mouth.

However, we pass quickly over our manner of proceeding,
but you can gain more information from these devout men,
our monks, the bearers of this letter. A sermon was preached
on the first day, there, and having assumed as much
solemnity and reverence as we could, we obliged all the
monks to swear in the presence of the sacrament that they
would yield to the judgement of the Order over the crimes
they had committed and would never again in future conspire
against the Order and their mother-house Clairvaux or the
visitors acting on their behalf, and would not give counsel,
help, or support to conspirators; then all were solemnly and
devoutly absolved in the sanctuary in the presence of the
Lord's body so that the enormity of their guilt would in
some way burst before them from the impressiveness of this
act, and we immediately proceeded to take the necessary
steps for the appointment of an abbot so that they would not
perchance have the opportunity to call in those rapacious
robbers, their relations, and prepare some evil plots in their
usual manner against our proceedings. At length, despite the
arguments of those seeking delay there was promoted to abbot, through the grace of God and a great concern for vigi-
lance, a prudent and religious man of the Order, quite
well-known in the kingdom of France, namely the prior of
Beaubec,[6] Jocelyn by name. And so, for seven whole days

we devoted ourselves energetically and continuously, although with proper modesty and discretion, to the visitation and reformation of the house and the correction of faults, thoroughly examining in addition the charter of the abbot of Froidmont[7] in the hearing of all, and with the agreement of all we allowed the twelve monks and sixteen lay-brothers least at fault back into the monastery for the sake of peace, and we reconciled the remainder, around about forty fugitives, to the Order and sent them for punishment to monasteries throughout the realms of France and England, never to return except with your special permission. If it please you, Your Holy and Discreet Paternity should not give permission to return for any reason or for any request, either through yourself or through others or through letters, to anyone who has been expelled, but in the houses to which they were sent they should live and die. For now the monastery of Mellifont, being free of the useless and malicious for the greater part, can gradually receive upright and patient men sent there from your side, through whom the religious life will be established there.

The aforesaid house already begins to calm down a little and to show some signs of life. But should it happen that the aforesaid expelled members return, then the abbot will certainly retire whether we want it or not, and you will not again find a suitable person who will serve as abbot there and will competently fulfill the office of visitor, and the last errors will be worse than the first.[8] However, some of them, as we have ascertained, are going to the gates of Clairvaux to address you and your holy community, promising whatever you want; in regard to them, it is necessary that you prepare yourself lest perhaps under the appearance of mercy the discipline of the Order be dissolved and religious life perish. Almost everywhere these days greediness and shiftless dissoluteness is pursued in our Order. Whatever it demands, alleging mercy, is called mercy as an abuse unless it be granted. Mercy, that is, the heart of misery[9] today is, as it were, tying the Order in knots and dragging it to misery, concerning which it is said in the Proverbs: 'Justice elevates a people, sin makes a people wretched'.[10]

Further, Venerable Father, with your authority and that of the General Chapter, we decreed everywhere throughout Ireland that no one is to be admitted as a monk for any reason in future unless he knows how to confess his faults in French or Latin. Consequently, the Rule is now expounded only in French at Mellifont and your other daughter-house of Bective, as well as in many other houses of Ireland, and it will not be expounded otherwise in future, so that when you come personally or send visitors on your behalf they will understand those they are visiting and they will be understood by them, so that henceforth the less well-ordered will not take glee in finding a hidingplace under the cover of an unknown language. How can anyone love cloister or Writ who knows nothing but Irish? It is impossible to construct anything but a tower of Babel when the disciple does not understand the master, or vice versa, and cannot distinguish properly so that when one asks for bread, the other proffers a stone in place of bread and for fish gives a serpent.[11] For this reason, we have enjoined upon the Irish that, if they want to receive any of their people into the Order in future, they should send them to Paris or Oxford or other famous cities where they will learn letters and skill in speech and ordered habits, and we pointed out to them very clearly that the Order does not intend to exclude any race but only the inadequate, useless, and uncivilized; whereupon, God be blessed, they complied with this quite reasonably and sufficiently. Further, Beloved Father, we have confided certain secrets to the lips of the bearers of this letter to be reported at greater length to Your Holiness. If it please you, kindly give absolute trust to them and apply the corrective remedy for the salvation of souls and the honor of the Order

If I may be permitted to speak further to Your Paternity, for the authority of our Order and the zeal for souls with which we know you to be enflamed begets this audacity; the lack of persons of character is threatening our way of life with ruin and death, and deservedly so. Therefore, Venerable Father, it is in future principally your responsibility to find people who when put in control will stand out as pillars of the bowing walls of our Order and a framework nearly crumbling into ruins, and will attract, if not a large number, then at least a goodly supply of men who are praiseworthy for their life and for their learning, as it was in the time of Blessed Bernard, and who, when the time comes, will provide their support to our already ageing and tottering Order. Recall this further to mind because a wise king is the support of his people while wicked kings are the ruin of men.[12] Farewell.

1.   *Registrum,* No. XXXVII.
2.   From Dublin in early August, but after August 2; Abbot Stephen had remained at Mellifont until August 2.
3.   The visitors in 1227 had appointed R., a monk of Clairvaux, as Abbot of Mellifont; there is no record of his name; see Fr Colmcille, 'The Abbatial Succession at Mellifont, 1142-1539' in *County Louth Archaeological Journal* 15:1 (1961) 30-31.
4.   27 July 1228.
5.   Cf. Is 45:8.
6.   Beaubec (Bellus Beccus) in the diocese of Rouen, France, a daughter-house of Savigny: Janauschek, 96.
7.   The abbot of Froidmont, in the diocese of Beauvais, France, carried out the visitation of Mellifont in 1227, when the abbot of Mellifont was deposed: *Statuta,* 2:50.
8.   Qo 10:13.
9.   *misericordia, id est miserie corda*
10.   Pr 14:34.
11.   Cf. Mt 7:9-10, Lk 11:11-12.
12.   Cf. Ws 6:26, Pr 28:12.

28 [1]

TO THE ABBOT OF TROIS FONTAINES,[2] greetings. We do not hesitate to write with great confidence to Your Prudence concerning the matters of Ireland, so regretted by everyone, because you have received proof of their enormities and ignominous crimes through the evidence in part of your close associates and in part of your own eyes. Venerable Father, immediately after the departure of the abbot of Froidmont the aforesaid sinful race and worthless seed rose up on all sides against his orders; they treated with derision and spurned the decrees and punishments he had imposed on those who violated their duty and day after day they rashly heaped crime upon crime. Consequently, many monasteries claimed to be under no obligation to receive a visitation through him, but united in evil, they completely rejected the visitor sent to them, claiming that he had no juridical power whatsoever. Indeed, as late as last winter they also inflicted the greatest injuries on the abbot of Owney, whom the aforesaid lord abbot of Froidmont had appointed as his representative in these parts. His horses were secretly stolen, his cattle plundered, and some of his servants were killed, and it is said that this was done at their instigation out of hatred of and reproach to the visitors.

Furthermore, when the abbot of Baltinglass, who was the only one appointed from the other people,[3] returned to the monastery on the day of the Exaltation of the Holy Cross, he was thrown from his horse in a disgraceful manner by his own monks and lay-brothers in front of the gates of the monastery, and his seal was violently snatched from his belt and he was shamefully expelled in the midst of a great commotion; nor did he succeed afterwards in returning except in a throng of armed men. The abbot of Bective, who is also of the other language and people,[4] just succeeded, through the fear and terror of Lord W. de Lacy,[5] in remaining in his own house until our coming. Consequently, no one could describe within the space of a letter the labors and sorrows as well as the mortal dangers we are continuously exposed to for the honor of religious life and the laws of our fathers. Therefore, to only give a brief summary here, we have confided what remains in connection with the matter of the Irish and the changes we have made there on the advice of prudent men to the lips of the bearers of this letter, to be reported at greater length to Your Sincerity. Accept them, highly recommended, if it please you, and give a favorable hearing to their supplications. In addition, your zeal and religious devotion will not allow you to refuse to speak in the Chapter for the cause of the Order and the aforesaid matter, above all when it has been especially through your counsel and advocacy that the burden of the aforesaid labors, heavy and exceeding the measure of our strength, has been imposed on our shoulders,[6] and has been accepted by us. Farewell.

---

1.   *Registrum,* No. XXXVIII.
2.   August, from Dublin. Trois Fontaines *(Tres Fontes)* was in the diocese of Châlon-sur-Marne, and was the first daughter-house of Clairvaux: Janauschek, 7. The abbot of Trois Fontaines, together with the abbot of Froidmont, had carried out the visitation of the Cistercian monasteries in Ireland in 1227.
3.   The French-speaking Anglo-Normans in Ireland.
4.   The abbot of Bective, appointed by the visitors in 1227, had previously been a monk of Beaubec in France: Letter 59.
5.   Walter de Lacy, Lord of Meath; Bective was in county Meath, about four miles from de Lacy's great castle at Trim.
6.   The abbot of Trois Fontaines had recommended to the abbot of Clairvaux that Abbot Stephen should succeed him as visitor of the Irish monasteries.

29[1]

TO THE ABBOT OF CITEAUX,[2] greetings.
We have read your command, presented to us by Brother Vincent, with the respect it deserves, and are prepared to comply in all we can with the orders of Your Holy Paternity. Consequently, we have immediately added a companion to the aforesaid monk, a devout man, diligent and experienced in matters of this kind, namely the cantor of Duiske, who will go with him as an inseparable companion and a faithful ally through deserted and trackless lands where the aforesaid Brother Vincent has often exposed himself to countless mortal dangers, and still exposes himself for the sake of the duties enjoined on him, that they produce the due result. For which reason, we desire his devotion and the earnestness of his obedience to receive much commendation in the presence of Your Holiness, no matter what in the past some jealous people who lack the spirit of purity have perhaps complained about his actions in these parts, or have falsely laid accusations in secret; we speak the truth before God by the witness of conscience that, about both the falsification of your seal and the fraudulence with which [he was accused] by jealous prelates because of the urgings of their own guilt, we made a careful investigation for the honor of the Order and the protection of the innocent, among the abbots and monks with whom he had been in contact on his journey, or with whom he had tarried for a time, and his innocence was unanimously attested to by everyone under oath, quite apart from any insistence or knowledge of the same, and he was spoken of in a praiseworthy manner everywhere.

Consequently, if Your Prudent and Holy Paternity is willing to consent, many monasteries in Ireland would choose him with complete devotion and would earnestly request him to be appointed their father abbot. Very truly, Venerable Father, attempting to solicit the willing consent of Your Grace, we await your decision in this regard, and we request a reply in these and all other matters which we trust may redound to your honor and advantage in Christ, acting with a spirit of readiness, joy, and devotion; we send the bearers of this letter concerning the matters of the Irish, wretched and unheard-of in our Order, to the feet of Your Holy Paternity. Kindly receive them, if it please you, with the accustomed sweetness of your affection, and give a favorable hearing to them for the praise of God and the glory of both the head and the members. Farewell.

---

1. *Registrum,* No. XXXIX.
2. August, from Dublin.

30 [1]

TO R., BY THE GRACE OF GOD BISHOP OF SALIS-
BURY,[2] greetings.

Venerable Father, we would consider ourselves fortunate
if we were allowed the pleasure of sharing the labors and
sorrows to which we are continuously exposed for Christ and
the law of our fathers with so dear a friend as is he on whom,
after God, we depend solely and uniquely before all other
men. When we have the opportunity of meeting, his
presence is always pleasing, an acceptable consolation, his
words gentle, his love sweet, a coming together in Christ
Jesus delightful more than honey and honeycomb;[3] and this
is to my languishing spirit none other than an oil of refreshment and a spiritual unction, the only remedy in sorrow, a
refuge in persecution, more than all else a resting place in
labor; we speak the truth before God with the witness of
conscience that we receive your counsel as none other than
an expression of the divine will. Strengthened by your pro-
found maturity as by a strongly fortified tower, we fear not
the detraction and hatred of false brethren; on the contrary,
had it been required, we would not have feared even mortal
dangers, having always a ready heart and an eager will both
to serve your honor and to bear the burden with you,
thinking in this to be offering a sweet-smelling[4] sacrifice to
God himself.[5]

And still the recent and living memory of you is alive
before God in the recesses of our heart, and it is as if we saw
your face in person with our own eyes; if indeed Your Holy
Paternity responds to us in the same manner, if he is not
forgetful of us, he is marked with the stamp of that master
who, when he loved his own, he loved them even until the
end.[6] Venerable Lord, already we can say with the psalmist:

74

We are delivered the whole day into the hands of our mortal enemies, so that already we properly reckon ourselves as sheep marked down for the slaughter.[7] But for the sake of the Lord and for the purgation of sins we are prepared, with his help, to bear everything not only patiently but also joyfully, keeping in mind that the present life is but smoke that last for a little while, and joy which shines with the appearance of a moment.[8] Truly the labor of good men is a noble harvest, and it does not fail but remains for eternity.[9] We trust indeed in the Lord Jesus that the light and momentary weight of our tribulations will produce for us the eternal weight of our glory.[10] For already, for his part, he has brought us by grace the pledges and first fruits of the spirit, because he has deigned to make us in some small way a sharer in his suffering. And furthermore because he has opened the hearts of the Irish to his law and to his precepts so that they make peace and turn their hearts at least a little to following in the footsteps of the fathers from whose paths they had, like alien children, wholly turned away.[11] Indeed, we have appointed many abbots there from the other language and people, in the midst of great and repeated mortal danger, abbots who are one and all vigorously laboring in the vineyard of the Lord and who consider our presence and the opportunity of our counsel and fellowship to be a consolation in tribulation when some misfortune breaks in, which misfortune does not cease to pour in every day like the tide of the sea.

On which account, by the command of the Order which we received recently, we will remain in the aforesaid country, having put aside any pretext or excuse whatever, until the feast of All Saints,[12] and we commit our house and sons in Christ to God and to the glorious Virgin and to your protection, counsel, and helpful advice; and, as you yourself well know, we are absolutely confident before all mortal men that your loving concern will prove itself in many ways through your unique ability. May the good Lord grant to you that he, the true sun, who has deigned to rise in your heart and to shed forth rays of light to his glory, praise, and honor, will never darken in your breast or be allowed to set. May Your Holy Paternity be well in the Lord, for just as by his grace we have loved one another together in life, so also in death before himself will we not be separated.

1.   *Registrum,* No. XL.
2.   August, from Dublin. The bishop of Salisbury was Richard Poore, translated from Chichester before 27 June 1217 and translated to Durham 14 May 1228: *Handbook of British Chronology,* p. 251. Abbot Stephen's monastery at Stanley was in the diocese of Salisbury. This letter was written before the news of the translation reached Stephen in Ireland.
3.   Ps 19:10.
4.   Ezek 16:19 *et alia.*
5.   Cf. Eph 5:2.
6.   Jn 13:1.
7.   Cf. Ps 44:22, Si 51:5.
8.   Cf. Jn 4:15, Jb 20:5.
9.   Cf. Ws 3:15.
10.   Cf. 2 Co 4:17.
11.   Cf. 2 S 22:45, 46.
12.   1 November.

31 [1]

TO THE ARCHDEACON OF WILTSHIRE,[2] greetings. We would consider ourselves fortunate if we were allowed the heart-felt joy of sharing the labors and sorrows to which we are continuously exposed for Christ and the law of our fathers with that friend on whom, after the lord bishop of Salisbury, we depend before all living men. His presence, when it is given to us, is always pleasing, the acceptable company, the coming together in the house of the Lord more delightful than honey and honeycomb.[3] Indeed, there still lives in our secret heart the recent and living memory, God knows, and it is as if we see your face present with our own eyes. Indeed, you will respond to us in the same way if you recall the life and teaching of Jesus Christ and continuously keep in mind that when he loved his own, he loved them until the end.[4] Venerable friend, already we can say with the psalmist: We are delivered the whole day into the hands of our mortal enemies etc.,[5] as in the preceding letter.[6] Farewell always in the Lord, who has given to us the hope that, just as we loved one another in life, so also in death we will never be separated from him.

---

1. *Registrum,* No. XLI.
2. August, from Dublin. Stanley Abbey was in Wiltshire.
3. Ps 19:10.
4. Jn 13:1.
5. Ps 44:22.
6. The remainder of Letter 30 after these words (excluding the conclusion) was included as well in this letter.

32 [1]

T O NOBLEMAN A. BASSET,[2] greetings.

For the support and friendship you display towards us and our house we offer our thanks and gratitude however small, devoutly praying that God will repay you and will make up for our insufficiency when the time comes. We sincerely desire that your state will in all things prosper and that of yours and of our special supporter and protector before God, even though our merits are slight or non-existent. And no doubt you wish the same for us. Know, therefore, that we labor continuously with all our strength for the honor of the Church and of our Order in the midst of great and repeated mortal danger, often threatened as much by Irish chieftains as by robbers. But the good and merciful Lord has protected us and ours from all this so far and has preserved us by his grace unharmed. It is not permitted to write at length concerning these things; we have enjoined the bearer of this letter to report them to you and to ask you as a dearly-beloved lord and guardian, with all the humility and devotion of which we are capable, to retain and preserve even until the end, if it please you, the affection and the love which you have long shown towards our house, so that God, when he comes at the most acceptable hour, will repay you as you deserve; and know for certain that in all the good works we do, and in all the tribulations and dangers of death we bear, we will be devoted and beholden to you and yours before God according as we are able. Farewell and for long.

---

1. *Registrum,* No. XLII.
2. August, from Dublin.

33

TO LORD J., SON OF PETER,[2] greetings.
We desire greatly and deservedly that everything which concerns you be preserved in goodness with God and prosperity with men inasmuch as you have decided to embrace us and our house with such strength of affection that you always number our successes among your own, while adversities, if they should befall us, offend and harm us no more than they do your devotion and in us and for us. Therefore, offering abundant thanks to God and to you, in so far as we can though not as we would wish, for the benefits and favors given, we pray that He may extend his hand to repay you and may make up for our insufficiency, concerning which the psalmist says: 'You have opened your hand' etc.[3] Therefore, dearly beloved friend, may you be prepared to bring what you have begun in and for Christ up to its final conclusion. Further, be it known to Your Beloved that we and ours, although well enough in bodily health, are exposed continuously to incessant labors and sorrows for the honor of the Church and of the Order, often over-burdened beyond the limit of our endurance so that we despair of life itself.[4] However, rejoicing only in hope,[5] may God be blessed in everything. For if we are dying then we will live, if we are enduring then we reign,[6] holding as certain that this is not a journey from delights to delights, but it is necessary to pass through fire and water and in this way to be brought to a place of refreshment.[7] We have entrusted the rest of our news to the bearer of this letter to report more clearly to Your Beloved. As those things will be described, we pass over them here to avoid the tedium of prolixity. We devoutly commend you then to God and to the glorious Virgin and to our blessed patrons Benedict and

Bernard, together with our very special friend the archdeacon of Wiltshire, who will guard you spotless from the world[8] although you remain in the world and will render you acceptable to God. Farewell.

1.   *Registrum,* No. XLIII.
2.   August, from Dublin. The recipient has not been identified.
3.   Ps 145:16.
4.   Cf. 2 Co 1:8.
5.   Cf. Rom 12:12.
6.   Cf. 2 Tm 2:11, 12.
7.   Cf. Ps 66:11.
8.   Cf. Jm 1:27.

34 [1]

TO LORD R. OF LEXINGTON,[2] greetings.

Be it known to Your Beloved that we are as safe and well as can be expected at present; nevertheless, because of sea-sickness and the enormous amount of work which followed, our body is rather weak; above all earthly concerns we long for your prosperity and your unfailing health of soul and body, which may God and our Lord Jesus increase from day to day.

Beloved brother, how often have we been exposed to the robbers, to the persecution of chieftains and to the malignant manoeuverings of false brethren for the honor of the Church and the renewal of the religious life. But the good Lord by his grace has freed us and ours so far from the hand of those seeking our life,[3] and has preserved us unharmed.[4] He has opened to us the way by which we believe we will tame the pride of the Irish monks and change their hearts for the better, unless certain deceitful men secretly oppose us whose names we pass on to you through the bearer of this letter. Because of all this, we still urgently require that the Lord King admonish by letter the Justiciar of Ireland to attend vigorously and effectively to our affairs, and especially those of our chancellor. We commend you, therefore, and everything which concerns you to God, and we commend our house of Stanley to you; for the sake of brotherly love, especially in our absence, may your help, advice, encouragement, and protection never be lacking to it in a time of necessity and in days of tribulation. We have passed on everything else which is related to our condition to the bearer of this letter, to report to Your Sincerity at greater length. Fare well and for long.

1.   *Registrum*, No. XLIV.
2.   August, from Dublin. Lord R. was the eldest brother of Abbot Stephen.
3.   Qo 51:5.
4.   Cf. Wis 19:6.

35 [1]

TO THE ABBOT OF KILBEGGAN, greetings.
We strictly command you by virtue of the obedience
by which you are bound to the Order, having put aside every
excuse or delay, to present yourself at Dublin on the vigil of
Blessed John [2] to deal with the difficult matters of the Order
together with us and with other abbots; and know for certain
that, however much we love you in the Lord, we will not be
able to consider your disobedience lightly if you fail to come
and, with the counsel of worthy men, we will punish you
deservedly for it. Farewell.

---

1. *Registrum,* No. XLV.
2. 23 June 1228.

36 [1]

TO THE ABBOT OF RIEVAULX,[2] greetings.
We transfer to the lap of Your Holiness the bearer of this letter, Brother R., formerly a fugitive from the Order but reconciled by us because of his obvious signs of repentance. Nourish him in your house among your sons for whatever time you consider to be most advantageous for the salvation of his soul. We entrust him to Your Beloved because he was a monk of that monastery[3] which was united to the daughter-house of our house in Ireland. Farewell.

---

1. *Registrum,* No. XLVI.
2. Rievaulx in the diocese of York, England, a daughter-house of Clairvaux: Janauschek, 22.
3. Killenny, which, by the decree of the General Chapter in 1227, was united to Duiske: *Statuta,* 2:62.

37 [1]

TO THE ABBOT OF LOOS,[2] greetings.

Having been sent with the grace of visitation to the region of Ireland at great expense and in repeated mortal danger, we are compelled to disperse many monks and lay-brothers of the aforesaid realm through the kingdom of France and through Wales, and to send them to ordered houses where they may have the necessities of life and may learn discipline. And so we direct the bearers of this letter to Your Holiness, asking and, by the authority of the General Chapter and of the lord abbot of Clairvaux, requiring you out of respect for them and in obedience to the Order, kindly to receive the aforesaid monks and to keep them in your house; do not send them back to the region of Ireland without the special permission of the lord abbot of Clairvaux, for it is in no way advantageous for the Order or for the salvation of souls. Let them take the lowest place of all for two years. Farewell.

---

1. *Registrum,* No. XLVII.
2. Loos (Laus B.M.V.) in the diocese of Tournai, France, a daughter-house of Clairvaux: Janauschek, 116.

38 [1]

TO THE PRIOR AND COMMUNITY OF BOYLE,[2] greetings.

Having taken the advice of men of authority and of the greatest experience, both religious and seculars, and having given careful consideration to the matter, we have assigned your house as a perpetual and rightful daughter-house of Clairvaux. Furthermore, on the day after the Blessed John the Baptist,[3] before all the abbots of Ireland in Chapter, we solemnly absolved in perpetuity all the professed of your house, both monks and lay-brothers, from every obedience and obligation which bound you to the monastery of Mellifont.

And so, for your salvation we admonish and strictly enjoin you by virtue of the obedience owing to the Order and the General Chapter and under penalty of excommunication to submit to the monastery of Clairvaux alone in future as your motherhouse in perpetuity, giving obedience with all devotion as sons of God and grace and not vessels of discord and dissension. We send to you, too, the bearer of this letter, Brother P., formerly Abbot of Kilbeggan, to whom we have passed on certain information to be imparted to your ear on our part. Trust him as completely as you would us. Further, the prior of the house and the master of lay-brothers will come to us with the aforesaid monk P., without refusal or delay, to the region of Dublin, to confer with us concerning the state of your house. Meanwhile, apply yourselves with such diligence to the ordering of your house both internally and externally that it will always be enlarged and increased in spiritualities and in temporalities. Farewell.

1.   *Registrum,* No. XLVIII.
2.   After June 25. The abbot of Boyle was deposed by the General Chapter of
1227 as one of the leaders of the Mellifont conspiracy: *Statuta* 2:61.
3.   25 June 1228.

39 [1]

To THE PRIOR AND COMMUNITY OF MONASTER-
EVIN,[2] greetings.

We have greatly desired to come to your house. However, we are detained at Dublin by difficult and very demanding affairs of the Order and we cannot come to you at this time. But we would have been very pleased and delighted if things were otherwise. Therefore, we have committed our powers of appointing an abbot in your house to the venerable men bearing this letter, strictly commanding you by virtue of the obedience which is owing to the Order and the General Chapter to obey them in all respects in this regard as you would us, knowing that we have given them the power of imposing sentence of excommunication and even more severe punishments on rebels and opponents, if the need arises. Therefore, so dispose yourselves in all respects as sons of peace and obedience that we ought to have your devotion worthily commended in the sight of God and men, and unless on account of your arrogance, may that never happen, it will be necessary for us to enforce our power in certain ways and to summon heaven and earth in deserved chastisement, that is to say, the divine vengeance and the secular arm. Farewell.

---

1. *Registrum,* No. XLIX.
2. Monasterevin (Rosglas), in the county of Kildare, county Kildare, a daughter-house of Baltinglass: Gwynn and Hadcock, p. 142.

40 [1]

TO THE ABBOT OF HOLM CULTRAM,[2] greetings. Since the General Chapter bestowed on us the power of adjudicating and arranging the affairs of the Order through all the houses of Ireland in whichever way we considered advantageous, and we decreed that monks and lay-brothers be sent to certain houses of the Order, we transfer to you Brother G., monk, the bearer of this letter, formerly a fugitive but now worthily penitent and reconciled by us to the Order, to stay with you on condition that he take the lowest place of all for a year, be on bread and water every Friday, and receive the discipline in chapter. Therefore, we order you by the authority of General Chapter and we admonish you to receive him kindly and to take charge of him honorably according to the Rule and discipline of the Order, not letting him return at any time to Irish parts without the special permission of the General Chapter. Farewell.

---

1. *Registrum,* No. L.
2. Holm Cultram in the diocese of Carlisle, England, a daughter-house of Melrose and mother-house of Grey Abbey, county Down, Ireland: Gwynn and Hadcock, p. 134.

4I [1]

TO THE PRIOR OF MELLIFONT,[2] greetings.

In consideration of the divine mercy and likewise of the petition, we would be very pleased to restore the bearer of the letter, monk A., to his house; but he is a fugitive and it is decreed concerning him in a charter sent to us that he is not to be reconciled to the Order except through the abbot of Clairvaux, nor is he to return to Mellifont except through the General Chapter. But being prepared at your insistence [to spare] [3] the infamous simple-wittedness and the devout contrition of this wretch, we have agreed to reconcile him by kindly dispensation to the Order and to his house, but with a penance outside the gate-house, in accordance with the discipline of the Order, in this manner: when he comes to the gate to make satisfaction, he is to return his habit to you and he is to be given a lay-brother's habit, and he is to be content with that for eight days. However, the habit which he deservedly lost because he was a fugitive is to be returned to him on the eighth day. And then again he is remain outside the entrance performing penance for a further eight days. With the passing of the fifteen days he is to enter the Chapter seeking mercy and is to remain in the lowest place of all until we come to you. Farewell.

---

1. *Registrum,* No. LI.
2. Before July 27.
3. There is a vacant space in the manuscript; one word appears to be missing; it may be *parcere: Registrum,* p. 57.

42 [1]

TO THE ABBOT AND COMMUNITY OF TRACTON, greetings.

We very strictly command you by virtue of the obedience which is owing to the Order and the General Chapter to receive kindly that devout man and praiseworthy religious, Brother W., your monk, who has lived for quite a long time in the house of Bective, and he is to remain with you in perpetuity as in his own house notwithstanding any prohibition of the father-abbot or of anyone else, and having once received him you will kindly deal with him all the days of his life. [2]

In addition, on the above-mentioned authority under penalty of deposition or expulsion, we prohibit you from ever receiving anyone as a monk unless he knows how to confess his faults in French or Latin. We do not intend with this decree to exclude any people, whether English, Scots, Welsh, or Irish, but only persons who are unsuitable for and completely unproductive to the Order. For how can anyone love the Order or observe the seriousness of the silence or the discipline of the cloister who does not know how to find any consolation at all in the Scriptures, or to meditate even a little on the law of God either by day or by night? [3]

Further, we strictly decree under the same penalty that the Rule, which ought to be uniformly expounded and observed by everyone, is to be expounded only in French [4] in future so that the disorderly cannot hide themselves when visitors come with the authority of the General Chapter or of our venerable motherhouse at Clairvaux, but all will understand and will be understood by all; this will make it possible for faults to be dealt with properly and ignorant persons beneficially instructed, for otherwise the aforesaid visitors will waste their time building a tower of Babel in the confusion of languages where one seeks in his own language for bread and the other in his own idiom offers him a scorpion in place of bread.[5] No-one could estimate how many evils have arisen from this, and how many disorders remain unpunished under such circumstances. Furthermore, if a monk or lay-brother commits a fault which merits his being sent out or expelled, in no instance will he be transferred to another house in Ireland but to a house of another realm where he may be properly provided for and may learn discipline. For he cannot be disciplined in accordance with his needs in the aforesaid realm when either provisions are completely lacking or where houses are overwhelmed by an abundance of debts. Farewell.

---

1.   *Registrum,* No. LII.
2.   Cf. Pr 31:12.
3.   Ps 1:2.
4.   Tracton was a Welsh-speaking monastery: see Letter 98.
5.   Cf. Lk 11:12.

43 [1]

T O THE ABBOT AND COMMUNITY OF KNOCKMOY, greetings.

With the firm and unanimous advice of men of authority and of the greatest experience, both religious and secular, etc., as in the letter concerning Boyle in the preceding folio down to: not vessels of discord and dissension.[2] In respect of the lands, do not completely alienate the whole of them but for the promotion of your house etc. in order.[3]

---

1. *Registrum,* No. LIII.
2. Letter 37, excluding the sentences referring to Brother P., former Abbot of Kilbeggan, was repeated in this Letter.
3. The letter concludes with the words: *De terris vero nichil omnino alienetis, sed domus vestre promotione et cetera ut st: Registrum,* p. 58.

44 [1]

To W., PH. AND T., Abbots of Maigue,[2] Jerpoint, and Duiske, greetings.

The Beloved in Christ, Lord M., Abbot of Baltinglass, came to us and devoutly maintained that he believed it would greatly benefit the salvation of his soul for him to serve God and the Order elsewhere than in the aforesaid house. Wherefore, graciously acceding to his request and desiring in everything his salvation and honor, we order each and every one of you with the authority of the Order and of the General Chapter to accept his resignation with all respect and veneration, providing for him honorably and respectfully as a devout and venerable man so that we may worthily commend your diligence. Also accept the resignation of Abbeyleix,[2] as we have the mandate from the General Chapter concerning this, and immediately make provision in accordance with the honor of God and of the Order according to the procedure of which you will be notified for the house of Monasterevin and that of Baltinglass, concerning the father and pastor. At the same time, appoint an abbot at Abbeyleix, having God and the discipline of the Order before your eyes. By the authority of this present letter, we also order the communities of Baltinglass, Monasterevin, and Abbeyleix to obey you or any of you just as they would us. For we confer on you the full power of administering punishment to rebels and of compelling elected officials to submit to you. Therefore, let them so conduct themselves in all respects as sons of peace and obedience that we may commend their devotion deservedly, and not be obliged to use our power more severely against the rebellion of the same—may it never happen—and to summon heaven and earth, that is the divine vengeance and the secular arm, against them. Farewell.

1.   *Registrum,* No. LIV.
2.   Abbeyleix (Leix, Lex Dei) in the diocese of Leighlin, county Laois, a daughter-house of Baltinglass: Gwynn and Hadcock, p. 124.

45 [1]

T O THE PRIOR OF BEAUBEC, [2] greetings.

Being desirous, God knows, to act in accordance with your wishes, we arranged to make a journey to Mullingar [3] on Tuesday, but we are detained by regalian as well as episcopal matters and cannot depart from Dublin before the council is concluded on account of various dangers which are threatening between kingship and priesthood. Wherefore, we pray Your Beloved to excuse our absence at this time, knowing for certain that unless some new and unexpected difficulty occurs, we will make our way, the Lord granting, to the lord bishop of Meath and to yourself for your business immediately after the council. Farewell.

---

1. *Registrum,* No. LV.
2. From Dublin, before 20 July. The prior was Jocelyn, whom Abbot Stephen installed as abbot of Mellifont in his visitation which commenced on 27 July.
3. Mullingar, the cathedral town of the diocese of Meath, is situated fifty miles north-west of Dublin; the bishop of Meath was to attend the meeting: see Letter 47.

46 [1]

To MASTER E. OF DURHAM, greetings.

As we have cherished you amongst our special friends in the depths of our heart, according to our capacity, from our first acquaintance, we pray with so much the more solicitude and devotion that your position will always be maintained in prosperity. In relation to this, we fear much disturbance on account of the sad and tearfully lamented translation of our very great and well-beloved friend, formerly Bishop of Salisbury.[2] Indeed, his memory does not cease to be a continuous sorrow for us; for this reason, reverend friend, we few who are left, although widely separated in body and realm, ought to be very sincerely and firmly rooted and joined together with our whole heart and mind in the love of Christ. We in Ireland, weakened by tribulations and surrounded on all sides by a sea of dangers, humbly and devoutly pray to the Most High, which is all we can do, that the good Lord, who in his kindly compassion has caused us to be united in his love, will also through his gracious favor make us companions together in the enjoyment of his kingdom. Farewell.

We are safe and unharmed, though in the midst of continuous dangers from robbers and false brethren lying in ambush for our blood day and night.

---

1. *Registrum,* No. LVI.
2. Richard Poore, translated to Durham in May 1228; see Letters 30, 31.

47[1]

TO THE BISHOP OF MEATH,[2] greetings.

We arranged to be at Mullingar in the presence of your Holy Paternity on the octave of the translation of Blessed Thomas the Martyr,[3] if it were pleasing to the Lord and were permitted by the unavoidable demands of our Order which detain us at Dublin while the council of the kingdom there assembled continues. Wherefore, having heard on many occasions of your goodness and kindness, acknowledging great trust in the Lord although not of our deserving, we humbly and devoutly request you with all the strength we can to postpone the business of the abbot and community of Beaubec until the Thursday immediately before the feast of St Mary Magdalen[3] for, the Lord willing, we wish to have on these and some other matters your conversation, counsel, and, if it please you, consolation in Christ. Farewell.

---

1.   *Registrum*, No. LVII.
2.   Dublin, before July 20. Ralph Petit was Bishop of Meath: *Handbook of British Chronology*, p. 319.
3.   July 7 was the Feast of the Translation of St Thomas Becket.
4.   20 July 1228. The feast was on 22 July.

48[1]

TO ALL THE FAITHFUL of Christ etc.

Be it known to all of you that with the authority given to us by the General Chapter we have fully commissioned the abbot of Maigue to accomplish the act of union of the house of Glanewydan with the house of Dunbrody, so that he can punish all rebels and resisters in accordance with what he considers advantageous. In witness of which matter etc.

---

1. *Registrum*, No. LVIII.

49¹

49 [1]

TO THE ARCHDEACON OF WILTSHIRE, greetings.
We would lament with anguish the translation of our
friend [2] and the disturbance of our house and of our other
friends if sorrow would give place to sorrow or wound to
wound.

Nevertheless, we rejoice in the hope and mercy of our
Maker who through these things and in this way admonishes
his adopted sons to spurn visible things and transfer our
thoughts to those things which are not seen, and to build
up merits there where everything is completely fixed and
unchangeable, and remains now as it was before. Most dearly
beloved friend, we always consider ourselves to be defaulting
debtors who are wholly insufficient in thanksgiving for your
proven affection. Yet, the loving Jesus Christ, in whom alone
the power and the will equally correspond, will repay with a
deserved reward the grace of your devotion, which you have
had for us from the very beginning of our coming to know
one another. We indeed plead with him to do so because our
spirit dissolves and fails at the name and memory of our most
beloved friend, formerly Bishop of Salisbury, and at the same
time at yours, so that truly your name is to us oil poured
out [4] in the love of Christ. There is, however, one temporal
matter on which we seek your help, counsel and, not least,
your consolation, and that of all men who are our friends:
this concerns the peace of our house and the customary
liberty of the forest, which should be striven for by you and
by all our friends in so far as they can. For we believe our
spirit will be quite unable to bear it with goodwill if we
should find on our return an intolerable disturbance which
would force us to new rushing around all over the place and
excessive labors after so much weariness of body and spirit;

rather it would be disposed to lead the remainder of life in subjection and obedience in some very remote and concealed place which our most sweet Lord will decree more in accordance with the salvation of our soul, and where he will draw our heart with the appeal of his inspiration. Farewell.

1.   *Registrum,* No. LIX.
2.   Richard Poore, Bishop of Salisbury, translated from Salisbury to Durham.
3.   Cf. 2 Cor 4:18.
4.   Sg 1:2.

50 [1]

T O THE PRIOR OF NEWRY,[2] greetings.

Since the established punishment for the transgression of your monk, the bearer of this letter, is expressly defined in the Usages, it was not necessary to consult us on this matter or to send the aforesaid monk on such a tiring journey to us. Wherefore, we order you by virtue of the obedience which is owing to the Order and the General Chapter to receive him kindly and, in accordance with the rules laid down in the Usages, to place him in the rank of penitent for the rest of his life, devoutly providing the necessities for him, and to impress this upon him, frequently refreshing him with the grace of consolation, so that he will be stronger in making satisfaction than ever he was in delinquency, and he will be as prepared to submit to anything for avoiding the death of the soul as he was to whatever he underwent for avoiding the death of the body; and apply yourself in all the ways you can in accordance with the advantage of the Order to make provision and to take precaution that he is not overwhelmed by excessive grief, encouraging him to patience and perseverance in true and humble penitence. For the sufferings of this time are not worthy to be compared with the future glory. Farewell.

---

1.   *Registrum,* No. LX.
2.   Newry (Viride Lignum) in the diocese of Dromore, county Down, a daughter-house of Mellifont: Gwynn and Hadcock, p. 142. The abbot of Newry was among the abbots deposed by the General Chapter of 1227: *Statuta,* 2:61.

51 [1]

TO THE PRIORS AND COMMUNITIES of Newry, Grey Abbey[2] and Cumber,[3] greetings.

We have greatly desired etc. as in the letter sent to the community of Monasterevin[4] with the addition of this clause: We have previously informed the aforesaid visitor of the procedure to be followed concerning the persons of those houses from whom you are free to make an election. It is not permitted to exceed the requirements of that mandate in any way. This commission was given to the abbot of Inch.[5]

---

1. *Registrum,* No. LXI.
2. In the manuscript this monastery is called 'Aranea', which Abbot Stephen would seem to have confused with Grey Abbey.
3. Cumber (Comber) in the diocese of Down, county Down, a daughter-house of Whitland: Gwynn and Hadcock, p. 130.
4. Letter 39.
5. *Insula Curcii* (Iniscourcey) in the diocese of Down, county Down, a daughter-house of Furness: Gwynn and Hadcock, p. 135.

52 [1]

TO THE KING OF CENEL EOGHAIN,[2] greetings.
At your insistence we have freed the bearers of this
letter from the chain of excommunication with which they
were bound and have reconciled them to the Order; accord-
ingly, they will be allowed back into the monastery of
Mellifont on condition that they bring back the cross,
chalices and charters which they took away with them,
together with certain books. In addition, as you requested,
we have kindly and through dispensation provided, with all
the honor we can and dare, according to the rules of our
Order, for all who went out from or were expelled from
Mellifont, that they never again be fugitives, no matter what
they claim to Your Excellency, unless they spurn our counsel
and refuse to obey the Order in future. For we admitted some
of them into the house of Mellifont out of great mercifulness
and against the statutes of our Order; we sent the others,
however, to other well-ordered and well-provisioned houses
to remain for a time there where they will be strengthened
in soul.

Therefore, we kindly beseech Your Reverence with all the
devotion we are capable of, for your perpetual honor and
safety of soul, to protect and defend the aforesaid house of
Mellifont, together with the abbot and the persons there
assembled, in the way which is proper for so great a prince,
never allowing anyone under your power and dominion to
harm the aforesaid house or persons or to molest it in any
way. May Your Highness know for certain that we have the
power and the mandate from the General Chapter as well as
from the lord abbot of Clairvaux that, if the house of
Mellifont is not prepared to be at peace or if it engaged in
any sort of rebellion against the Order in future as it has

been accustomed to do, we will make an exchange with the king or the marshall of the aforesaid monastery of Mellifont with all its lands and belongings, receiving land in return in a safe place, namely in England or Leinster, where the monastery can be completely re-built and a community sent wholly from Clairvaux; may God prevent this, nor would we ever require such a thing unless the unruliness of robbers or a fresh conspiracy of monks make it imperative and essential.

If it please you, then, graciously receive the aforesaid monks, the bearers of this letter, and return them, together with the goods of Mellifont which they carried away, to the aforesaid house at the proper time lest they lose the indulgence granted them on account of your petition and out of respect for you, and so that glory, praise and honor before God and men will deservedly increase to you and your kingdom on account of your devotion to God and the Order. Farewell.

---

1.   *Registrum,* No. LXII. From Mellifont, July 27—August 2, or from Dublin after August 2.
2.   While the identity of this king is not certain [see Colmcille, *Comhcheilg na Mainistreach Mhoire* p. 106] it was probably Aed O Neill, King of the Cenel Eoghain, whose obituary is given in the *Annals of Connacht* ed. A.M. Freeman (Dublin Institute for Advanced Studies, 1944), p. 39 (1230).

53[1]

TO THE BISHOP OF OSSORY,[2] greetings.

With all humility we kindly beseech Your Paternity to postpone the meeting arranged by us between yourself and the abbot and community of Jerpoint until the Saturday immediately before the Assumption of the Blessed Virgin, knowing for certain that we have not requested this delay by making excuses or on account of any negligence in this regard, but because the state of Mellifont, difficult and dangerous beyond measure as Your Prudence well knows, has caused us to be detained here longer than we had intended, having been variously entangled for seven days already in great distress and continuous mortal danger. For this reason, we have been deprived so far of the longed-for riches of your gracious presence. Therefore, may the kindness of Your Holy Paternity excuse my absence and, if it please you, arrange what we seek so that everything can be settled in that place where they were, namely, whatever concerns the house of Jerpoint.[3] If you agree, moreover, we will meet at Kilkenny[4] on the Saturday before the Assumption,[5] as mentioned above. Would you arrange that Master P. of Christ-church also be present on that day and place for your honor and the salvation of the souls of our flock and in respect of our devout petition, so that we and our sons in Christ, the abbot and community of Saint Saviour,[6] can have peace of mind. For we are ready to follow your counsel and arrangements in all respects, since no negotiation concerning servile status can intervene in spiritual matters, namely in resignations and things of the kind. We will carry out devoutly and without opposition, without any such negotiation, whatever you arrange and decree. For God knows we are concerned with great anxiety of heart for the aforesaid souls. Would you inform us of your pleasure in regard to this letter.

---

1.   *Registrum,* No. LXIII. From Mellifont, before August 2.

2.   Peter Mauveisin was Bishop of Ossory: *Handbook of British Chronology,* p. 341. Jerpoint was in the diocese of Ossory.

3.   The allusion is to Killenny, once a daughter-house of Jerpoint but then suppressed as an independent house and united to Duiske.

4.   Kilkenny, county Kilkenny, the cathedral town of the diocese of Ossory, is situated 73 miles south-west of Dublin.

5.   12 August 1228.

6.   Duiske.

54[1]

TO THE ABBOT OF BALTINGLASS, greetings.

When we were staying in the region of Mellifont, we heard from very many trustworthy and devoted religious that Brother T., your Great Cellarer, was, although secretly, the author and instigator of the whole horrible conspiracy which was so wickedly perpetrated against Lord M., his former abbot, to the scandal of the whole Order and to the perpetual notoriety of the aforesaid house. Wherefore, after having had much and deep consultation with many abbots and other worthy men, we command you by virtue of the obedience which is owing to the Order and the General Chapter, immediately these letters are received and putting aside every excuse and delay, to discharge the aforesaid T., your Cellarer, from his office and send him to the monastery of Fountains, never to return without the permission of the General Chapter. Thoroughly deceived, we had thought very different and better things of him for a long time. We grant by dispensation, however, that you include no punishment in his letter except that for a year he will take the lowest place among the priests. Or if he responds badly, send him to the monastery of Dieulacres[2] because you have one monk of theirs with you. To whichever place you send him, write saying that you have done this on our special command, knowing for certain that for as long as the aforesaid Brother T. remains in your monastery or granges after the reception of this mandate by the authority committed to us we place your church under interdict and we suspend you and your office-holders from the divine offices. Given at the monastery of Bective on the day after St Peter in Chains.[3]

1.   *Registrum,* No. LXIV.
2.   Dieulacres in the diocese of Coventry, England, a daughter-house of Combermere: Janauschek, 142.
3.   2 August 1228.

55[1]

TO THE ABBOT OF SHRULE, greetings.
We command you in virtue of the obedience you owe to the Order and the General Chapter, immediately this letter is received to proceed, with the subprior of Bective to visit on behalf of the lord abbot of Clairvaux the monasteries of Boyle and Knockmoy as rightful daughter-houses of Clairvaux. Appoint at Boyle an abbot in accordance with this instruction: give the electors[2] the choice of one out of the four persons whose names we write here. Two of them are English, two Irish: namely Nigel, Prior of St Mary's Abbey, Dublin; T., Cantor of Duiske; Nehemias, Prior of Mellifont; Constantine, monk of Maigue, formerly Abbot of Holy Cross. Although we had proposed at another time to promote Brother Donatus of Mellifont, it had not then come to our attention that he was named among the Mellifont conspirators. It is expressly prohibited for any of those to be appointed abbot for any reason. But if you find them rebellious —that is, the prior or anyone else—depose them immediately from their offices and if necessary excommunicate them, reporting their names back to us so that we can properly punish them. But we trust in the Lord Jesus concerning their discretion and holy religion that they will show themselves devout and obedient to you in all respects out of reverence for the Order and their mother Clairvaux, whom you represent. Show this letter to the electors. Farewell.

We have signed and sealed a charter which is to be read during your visitation and distributed, one copy to Boyle and another to Knockmoy, and is to be very carefully observed in future. Let monks and lay-brothers guard themselves against negligence because we send a copy to Clairvaux. Farewell.

1. *Registrum,* No. LXVI.
2. Only some members of the community had the right to vote at abbatial elections. In Ireland Abbot Stephen followed the established practice of arranging elections by appointing electors beforehand.

56[1]

T O ALL THE FAITHFUL of Christ etc.
We wish to bring to your notice that with the authority of the General Chapter given to us we have committed to Lord S., Abbot of Buildwas, full powers of visitation, correction and compulsion, according to what he considers advantageous, over all the houses established in Meath, Uriel,[2] and in the bishoprics of Kildare and Leighlin.[3] For we are obliged to devote ourselves in person with all the diligence of which we are capable to the visitation and to the reformation, with the help of God, of the monasteries of Munster.[4] In witness of which matter etc.

---

1.   *Registrum,* No. LXVI.
2.   Uriel is present-day county Louth; the monasteries in the commission for Meath and Uriel were Kilbeggan, Shrule, and Abbeylara; Bective and Mellifont, where Abbot Stephen had conducted the official visitations, were excluded. Abbeylara in the diocese of Ardagh, county Longford, was a daughter-house of St Mary's Abbey, Dublin: Gwynn and Hadcock, p. 124.
3.   Abbeyleix, Duiske, Baltinglass and Monasterevin were in the two bishoprics.
4.   Munster is the southern province of Ireland and included the monasteries of Kilcooly, Holy Cross, Owney, Odorney, Maigue, Suir, Fermoy, Chore, Tracton, Abbeymahon and Corcomroe.

57[1]

To THE VENERABLE LORD BISHOP OF SALISBURY,[2] greetings.

We kindly appeal to your Paternity on behalf of the prior of Mellifont, elected to the bishopric of Clogher,[3] who deserves commendation on account of his pleasing manners and moderate literacy, that you will promote his cause and this matter according to God. For the aforesaid bishopric is situated for the most part among mere Irish.[4] Do this much, if it please you, so that God will repay you as you deserve in due time and place. Farewell.

---

1. *Registrum*, No. LXVII.
2. Robert Bingham was elected Bishop of Salisbury after 25 September 1228, and consecrated 27 May 1229: *Handbook of British Chronology*, p. 251; this letter may have been addressed to his predecessor, Richard Poore.
3. Nehemias O Broghan was Bishop-elect of Clogher: Gwynn and Hadcock, p. 63. His name was among those from whom the electors at Boyle were to choose their abbot: Letter 55.
4. This term, *puri Hibernici*, was used by the Anglo-Normans as a synonym for the native Irish; it remained in use throughout the medieval period.

58 [1]

TO THE ABBOT OF MELLIFONT, greetings.

We command you by virtue of the obedience you owe to the Order and the General Chapter to sell your house which is within the enclosure of the nuns, according as it is convenient to do so. For it is quite contrary to the interests of your abbey to retain this on account of the scandal and shame of the Order and the wasting of your house through useless and improper expense, for which the before-mentioned place has so far provided opportunity and has created the risk of serious disgrace for the Order and your house. Turn what you get from the aforesaid sale to advantageous and useful purposes.

In addition, we require you by the same authority to absolve on our behalf with all solemnity and reverence all the fugitives of your house, monks and lay-brothers, who are penitent and seek mercy, that they may understand from the ceremony of absolution itself just how serious and how enormous was their offence and may in future be watchful. First of all, have them make a solemn promise, sworn over the holy relics in the presence of many people, never to hatch a conspiracy in future and never to give advice, help or support to those who do either in secret or in public against the Order, their mother Clairvaux, the visitors, or their own abbots. Having done this, provide them with letters for houses throughout the kingdom of France which are particularly suitable for such people, [stipulating that] they are never to return without the special permission of the lord abbot of Clairvaux. Do not send anyone to us for we are preparing to set off to the very remote region of Munster. But carefully note down the names of those sent out, who they are and to which houses they are sent, and carefully preserve the record of this so that we or other visitors can judge from it whether they are worthily and devoutly carrying out the penance imposed on them. In witness of which matter etc.

---

1.   *Registrum*, No. LXVIII.

59[1]

TO THE ABBOT OF FOUNTAINS,[2] greetings.

The abbacy of St Mary's Abbey, Dublin, having been made vacant through the voluntary resignation of Brother A., formerly abbot of the same, the monks of that house, proceeding in all respects according to the rules of the Order and with their mind's eye turned towards God alone, as we are undoubtedly convinced, made unanimous choice of Brother S. de Chatriz, your monk, who for a brief period took the place of the cellarer in your house, and they elected him as their father and pastor without any coercion or pressure by us or the father-abbot,[3] who were there present, in respect of the foresaid position of the same, but only with free election of members of four houses, Buildwas, the mother-house, Combermere,[4] Fountains, and Wardon;[5] having been given to them; we are convinced without doubt that this was brought about by divine Providence, who willed the appointment in the aforesaid house such a man, through whom counsel and help can be provided for your daughter-houses in Ireland and honor and glory be increased for all the Order established throughout Ireland. Wherefore, we earnestly entreat the discreet prudence of Your Holiness, and in the strength of the Holy Spirit we firmly implore you not to attempt on any account to impede the aforementioned brother, so necessary to the Order, whose foundation and cause, we speak the truth, is God alone, lest perhaps, may it never happen, you appear to be resisting the ordinance of God. We are quite certain that [resistance] will be useless, nor can this plan and deed be destroyed, for it was made by the Lord, according to what is stated in the Acts of the Apostles.[6] Keep in mind the affair of the prophet Jonah, who had taken flight so as not to preach penitence in Nineveh according to the word of the Lord, but at last, by the wonderful intervention . . . [7] by God, first by him and then through him, divine Providence was fulfilled. For where will we go when we flee from his spirit and where from his face?[8] Take care for your house, then, and let the aforesaid Brother S. take care lest perhaps the Lord allow a typhoon wind to arise and beat the ship of Fountains with storm-driven waves even to the point of sinking,[9] as happened to Jonah until he was ready to do His will. For his way is not as man sees it;[10] as is the will of God in heaven, so will it be done.[11] Therefore, may Your Holiness concede and consent and, making a virtue of necessity, may the before-mentioned Brother S. not refuse to undergo some little things for Christ who for him bore so much that was harsh, hard, and horrible. May he have compassion on his mother, our religious life, which bore him as well as us in Christ, which has nourished and supported us even until now, and now requests from her sons some return for that past time to her for all the things that she has rendered them.[12] Accepting, therefore, the cup of salvation for the sake of the Lord,[13] may he say with the Lord: 'Not as I will but as you'.[14] And even though both you and your community consider his labor essential to you, his counsel beneficial, his presence acceptable, his consolation sweet, still may you not deny his creature to Christ in whose hands are life and death.[15] Rather, rejoice the more if a shoot almost violently rooted out and ripped from you, if I may so describe it, is perchance planted anew in the vine-yard of the Lord Sabaoth, through which the old sterility will begin to flourish again and to send out fertile and fruitful progeny.

We ask you therefore, we admonish you by virtue of the obedience which is owing to the Order and the General Chapter and to your mother Clairvaux, the interest and the cause of which is principally carried out in this regard, and we firmly and strictly enjoin on you to send quickly the aforesaid man, who has been so sincerely and eagerly requested by all, to the aforesaid house of St Mary's, Dublin, kindly consigning him to the same, together with the bearers of this letter. For winter is close at hand[16] and delay brings danger. We send to you enclosed the seal of the aforesaid monastery under the seal of the father-abbot and our own. By giving this to the before-mentioned man solemnly in chapter, in accordance with the rules of the Order, with the authority of the Order and the father-abbot, you bestow on him the aforesaid burden and office by virtue of obedience and remission of sins, so that he may immediately receive the profession of the two monks bearing this letter. Therefore, following on the example of the visitors in Ireland in the previous year who absolved a monk of Clairvaux at Mellifont and a monk of Beaubec at Bective from their profession without having sought permission from their own abbots and appointed them to the position of abbot, and also observing the terms of our authority which freely allows us even to oblige priors for the advancement of the cause of Ireland to do likewise, we suspend at our will the frequently-mentioned S., your monk, from divine services unless he takes up the before-mentioned position, and if he puts it off beyond three days we excommunicate him with the authority of the Order and the General Chapter, and we denounce him for this to your community until such time as he comes to his senses and obeys the Order.

In addition, humbly prostrate at the feet of Your Piety and your community, we beg with tearful groans that you show a maternal heart towards your delicate and new daughters in future.[17] For, we speak of these things for your saving peace, the love you have shown them so far has been more lukewarm than it ought to be, and we say this with sorrow, it has represented more the indifference of a step-mother than the love of a mother. Because of this, your sons the abbots of Baltinglass and Jerpoint, venerable men and deserving of commendation before God and men, with great and frequent lamentation for the lack of help and counsel, cry out, 'Have pity, have pity, at least you, our friends[18] and fathers, because there is no-one else in this new state of things who succors us or provides for our safety'.

Further, the mouth of those that speak, I do not say wicked things,[19] but rather malicious things should not confuse or frighten you away because, the Lord willing, each of your daughter-houses will provide for itself in perpetuity within three years if it receives adequate help for two years from you; you can subject, reform, and visit the one through the other. Possessions truly pass away, but the salvation of souls remains for eternity.[20]

In addition, with the counsel of all the abbots of Ireland and on account of the horrendous and unheard-of conspiracy which the monks of Baltinglass infamously attempted against their own abbot in the past year, we have taken away from the same forever a better daughter-house, namely Monasterevin, for the restraint of the pride of the aforesaid house, and we have assigned it to you as a daughter-house to be held in perpetuity so that they will learn not to blaspheme from now on. We have threatened them with what we will do with what remains if they still turn their hand to evil.[21] Therefore, try to be the consolation not only by action but also by letter of the abbots of Jerpoint and Monasterevin and also the abbot of Baltinglass—who is favored before all other abbots in the opinion of the count of Bullii and the men of Leinster[22] and whom we put in command there on the advice of the abbot of Jerpoint as well as many others—lest, may it never happen, they be overwhelmed by excessive grief[23] on account of the immense labors and the lack of abundant solace. In truth, as God is our witness, we have been their one and only consolation so far in so far as we can. But we do not know what can be done for the future. For it is necessary for us to set out for the very remote houses of Ireland, to visit and reform them with the help of God; we do not know what the prudence of the divine dignity has prepared for us there concerning our life and safety. Farewell.

Have this letter read out carefully in the hearing both of your community and of the often-stated Brother S., your monk, devoutly commending to their prayers our danger, to which we are delivered in patience every day for the Order.

For we labor for them and their cause with the same devotion as for our own. Farewell.

---

1.   *Registrum,* No. LXIX. From Dublin, probably in September. Abbot Stephen returned to Dublin from Suir after completing his visitation on August 29 in order to conduct this election. He intended to return to Suir by September 29: Letter 66.

2.   John of Kent (1220-47).

3.   The abbot of Buildwas.

4.   Combermere in the diocese of Coventry, England, a daughter-house of Savigny: Janauschek, 100.

5.   Wardon in the diocese of Lincoln, England, a daughter-house of Rievaulx: Janauschek, 43.

6.   Ac 5:38.

7.   One or two words are illegible in the manuscript.

8.   Cf. Ps 139:6.

9.   Cf. Jon 1:4, Ac 27:14.

10.   Cf. Jer 10:23.

11.   1 M 3:60.

12.   Cf. Ps 116:11.

13.   Ps 116:12.

14.   Mt 26:39.

15.   Si 11:14, Pr 18:21.

16.   'Nam hiemps iminet in ianuis' suggests that the letter was probably written in September: *Registrum,* p. 68.

17.   Baltinglass and Jerpoint in 1227 and Monasterevin in 1228 were transferred as daughter-houses to Fountains: see Letter 22.

18.   Cf. Jb 19:21.

19.   Cf. Ps 63:12.

20.   Cf. 1 P 1:25.

21.   Cf. Is 5:25 etc.

22.   Leinster is the east-central province of Ireland, and included the monasteries of St Mary's Abbey, Dublin, Monasterevin, Baltinglass, Abbeyleix, Duiske, Jerpoint, Dunbrody, and Tintern Minor.

23.   Cf. RB 27:4.

60[1]

TO THE ABBOT OF MAN,[2] greetings.
We trust that Your Prudence is aware that the
monasteries of Ireland do not have the means to provide for
themselves and, with the authority of the General Chapter,
monks and lay-brothers have been and have to be dispersed.
Consequently, taking into account the needs and poverty of
the Order in the aforesaid land, we are compelled, although
reluctantly, to send back to you, his own pastor, your
sheep, namely the monk bearing this letter. See to it that he
is provided for as befits a spiritual son in another region, as
you consider advantageous. Farewell.

---

1. *Registrum,* No. LXX.
2. Rushden Abbey on the Isle of Man, between Ireland and England, a
daughter-house of Furness: Janauschek, 101.

61 [1]

T O THE COMMUNITY OF SUIR,[2] greetings.
Wounded inwardly by great sorrow of heart and deep regrets, we are not a little dismayed that that foundation which our holy fathers most devoutly planted for the spreading of divine service and salvation of souls has been turned, we say sorrowfully, into the scorn of seculars, the reproach of clerics, the talk of the world, and the ruin of the Order. Who therefore will give water to our head and a fountain of tears to our eyes[3] that we mourn not only the desiccation but also the sterility of the vine of the saints, which once put forth leaves, bloomed, and produced a copious supply of good fruits? In what way has the gold of holy religious life been darkened, to what has changed the color of illustrious estimation, and why are the stones of the sanctuary scattered[4] through the woodland and glade? Return, we beg you, return, most dearly beloved brothers and sons of God, and learn that true wisdom dwells in the fear of God and in the marriage-bed of holy obedience. Brothers, consider a little more deeply how dangerously foolish is he who does not fear to rebel against the ordinances of the Order, disregarding the fear of God. Whatever has been done among you so far without prudence and without reverence, for all that, as God is our witness, we desire with kindly piety, in a spirit of gentleness, to take care of and provide for you as brothers in so far as we can and ought.

Therefore, learn discipline lest at any time the Lord rage in his anger and you perish utterly from the just way.[5] This we admonish, that we beg, and we firmly entreat you in the Holy Spirit with all the authority of which we are capable to act so obediently, humbly, and reverently to the Order in these matters in future, and so to restrain the wickedness of those lacking in prudence, that the sincerity of your devotion and the labor of humble solicitude may shine through the result. For the house of Mellifont, and all the others who have already had their eyes opened by their misfortune, are there giving all their attention so that in as much as by their insolent obedience they saddened their mother, the Cistercian Order, and the Church of God, so to that extent they are striving to edify and to make her joyful by their humble and ready repentance. May the kind and merciful Lord, who alone can, likewise achieve the same result within your community. Therefore, if you are agreeable in Christ to obey the Order in future, which we firmly believe, write in reply to us through the bearer of this letter, sending two of the more senior members of your house so that we can have very careful and full consultation with them concerning the condition of the same. Farewell.

---

1.   *Registrum,* No. LXXI.
2.   Late August, from Jerpoint or Duiske.
3.   Jer 9:1.
4.   Lam 4:1.
5.   Cf. Ps 2:12.

62[1]

AGAIN TO THE COMMUNITY OF SUIR,[2] greetings.
Your Devotion has implored us through Brother J.,
your monk, the bearer of this letter, to delay our coming to
your house until the arrival of the Justiciar.[3] Indeed, we would
kindly agree to your request if there was any reason why it
should be granted. But before we received your letter we
had summoned many abbots to come to your house, and
with their counsel as well as with your own we might engage
in the reformation of your house as we can and ought, in
accordance with the office enjoined on us. For we are not
prepared to arrange or to dispose of anything on our own as
if we alone were deciding; but our preparedness is from God[4]
and from the counsel of prudent and God-fearing men. In
addition, the [time of] arrival of the Justiciar is not certain,
while this matter requires instant attention and delay produces danger. Consequently, we have arranged, the Lord
willing, to come to your house on a day within the week
immediately after the feast of St Bartholomew.[5]

Be prepared in true repentance as sons of God and not
vessels of discord or dissension to take up again very
earnestly the powerful weapons of obedience, namely patience and humility and the others, as the apostle writes,[6] if
by chance you have foolishly thrown these away at any
time, or if perhaps you have made use of them with but
little fervor. Direct the gaze of your mind to God alone and
to the patrons of our Order, Blessed Benedict and Bernard,
and so meditate on these that the attention of your heart is
fixed not on things which are visible but on those which are
invisible. For visible things are temporal while those which
are invisible are eternal, either in the punishment of hell or
the glory of heaven.

Be prepared at the same time to encourage the beloved in Christ, Brother D., your prior, to be of devout mind, for which we kindly supplicate with the Most High, that in mercy and compassion the kind and merciful Lord may remember him and draw his heart to a perfect knowledge of Himself and to true and humble repentance. For indeed, although he has departed with the prodigal son for a distant country,[8] if he still returns to his heart and desires to be restored to grace with the Great Father, as is right and proper, we are prepared with all fondness to grant the grace of absolution to him and to restore him to the favor of the Order, and also, as God is our witness, to provide for his salvation of soul and peace of mind, with the counsel of worthy men, in as much as we can and ought. But let it not happen that a christian man, and especially a religious and a monk of the Cistercian Order which is accepted before God and the angels and is so resplendent with the fame of renown among men, that he neglect his Creator and the Order and fly for refuge and place his trust in secular power as if he were an apostate or an infidel. For it is much better to trust in the Lord than to trust in men,[9] and to put hope in the spiritual arrows of prayer rather than in perishable secular weapons. For it is written: An armed people without God is unarmed.[10] Again: The name of the Lord alone is a most strongly fortified tower, there the just man takes refuge and is freed.[11]

Brothers, consider with what danger you daily celebrate [the divine service], in what risk of soul you live daily while you are not fully in the grace of the Order. For God's sake, hasten from imminent shipwreck to the safe harbor of the Order, seek the cure for the former disease, give your attention to the Most High Father who is offering you the robe and ring,[12] look at your mother, the religious life, which has borne you in Christ, has nourished and nurtured you, and regard the sad and weeping bosom of mercy still opening wide to infants, that is, to humble penitents, and with all the bowels of compassion, with your whole heart and a willing soul, produce fruits worthy of repentance from now on. For we are preparing to visit you only in the simplicity of the

Order, not with secular power, being ready, if it please the Lord, not only to be bound but even to die in Jerusalem[13] for himself and the laws of our fathers, Saints Benedict and Bernard, just as we and our companions are obliged to do by virtue of obedience and remission of sins. For whatever befalls us while we follow the office of obedience will always be for our good. Death and life, peace and disturbance, all merit is ours for the present and for the future glory and the crown.

We draw each and all of these things to the attention of the beloved in Christ, Brother D., your prior, and, the Lord knows, we have not refrained from writing to him by name out of malice, for we would devoutly and kindly write a letter directly to him if it were allowed. If he comes to us in person, as we have ordered, we acknowledge with great trust in the help of God that we will make proper provision for his health of soul and peace of mind. But whatever you have failed to do so far, give attention to making up for this in the future. Farewell.

---

1. *Registrum,* No. LXXII.
2. Late August but before August 24, from Jerpoint or Duiske.
3. Richard de Burgh. See Letter 15, n. 5.
4. Cf. 2 Co 3:5.
5. 24 August.
6. Cf. 2 Cor 6:4-7.
7. 2 Co 4:18.
8. He 15:13.
9. Ps 118:8.
10. Source unknown.
11. Pr 18:10.
12. Cf. Lk 15:22.
13. Cf. Ac 21:13.

63[1]

TO THE ABBOT OF OWNEY,[2] greetings.

We will be at Clonmel[3] on Saturday immediately after the feast of St Bernard,[4] the Lord willing, for the purpose of reforming the house of Suir if it can be done, and appointing an abbot there with your advice, if it shall please God. However, we have learned from monks of the aforesaid house whom we summoned to us that the prior and all his accomplices are doing everything they can to rebel against the Order, and are abhorring no crime but are merely taking what is pleasing for what is permitted.

Wherefore, we order you by virtue of the obedience which is owing to the Order and the General Chapter to meet us there on the aforesaid day at the appointed time. Further, we have told many things to the bearer of the letter to be reported more secretly to you. Trust him completely as you would us in this regard. Act carefully and very secretly in whatever you say or do concerning this matter. Farewell.

---

1. *Registrum,* No. LXIII. From Jerpoint or Duiske, before August 26.
2. Owney (Abington) was in the diocese of Emly, county Limerick, a daughter-house of Furness: Gwynn and Hadcock, p. 126. The abbot of Owney would have accompanied Abbot Stephen on the visitation of Suir which is here being prepared for.
3. The town of Clonmel, county Tipperary, lies on the river Suir about two miles from the monastery of Suir.
4. 26 August. The feast falls on 20 August.

64[1]

T O THE ARCHBISHOP OF CASHEL,[2] greetings.
We have told certain things to the bearer of the
letter, the monk Brother H., to be humbly reported to Your
Paternity. Be good enough to trust him completely and
kindly give a favorable hearing to him so that the diligence
and devotion which you have so far fervently displayed in
our regard for the advancement of the cause of the Order will
be brought to a better conclusion, and you will thence
deservedly receive glory, praise, and honor before God and
men. Farewell.

---

1.   *Registrum,* No. LXXIV. From Jerpoint or Duiske, before August 26.
2.   Abbot Stephen would have notified Archbishop Marianus O Briain through
the bearer of this letter about the impending visitation of Suir, due to com-
mence on 26 August. See also Letter 18, note. 2.

65[1]

To the abbot of fountains, greetings.

We are graciously sending Brothers M., formerly Subprior of Jerpoint, and M., monk, together with some other monks, to Your Holy Paternity; they have respectfully entreated us to transfer them to their mother-house for a period of time for the purpose of learning discipline and sound religious life. We desire them to have no little commendation as devout sons of a spiritual father. In addition, we ask Your Benevolence, and we affectionately admonish and firmly enjoin with the authority of the Order and of the General Chapter, that, treating them with fatherly affection, you keep them in your own house absolved of all sentences, as persons whom only the poverty of the aforesaid house and a desire for religious life bring humbly to you. Do not give them permission to return before two years have elapsed. But when this [time] has passed, grant them this graciously and readily.

Given at Jerpoint in the year of grace 1228, on the day after the Assumption of the Blessed Virgin.[2]

---

1. *Registrum,* No. LXXV.
2. 16 August.

66[1]

TO THE ABBOT OF SUIR,[2] greetings.

Being consoled in Christ who willingly endured so hard and so undeserved a death in shame contemptuous, do not absent yourself for any reason or go far away, especially in this new state of things, but always having God before your eyes, make no decisions in haste or precipitantly but [decide] everything with the counsel and the careful consideration of prudent and God-fearing men, and follow the counsel of Lord P. of Clonmel, seeking support and peace in gentleness and modesty in so far as you can from the bailiffs of the lord Justiciar and also of the other English and the Irish, returning harsh replies to no-one. Deal with your community with kindly instruction rather than with strictures on account of the long-standing disuse, endeavoring in so far as you can to be loved by them and by the men of the district, and while things are just beginning turn a blind eye to certain faults and disorders of theirs until such time as they can better understand and will be more capable. Do not receive Brother D., who was prior, into your house in future. If you consider it to be advantageous and if it will be for your peace, place old Brother J. in charge of the guest service, rejoicing always in the Lord that whatever befalls you or yours should be considered great gain, because you have been found worthy to bear reproach and hardship for the good of religious life. Farewell.

But, God willing and the route favorable, we shall come to your house with the grace of visitation around the feast of St Michael.[3] For the Justiciar will return from Connacht[4] around that time. Do not disparage or speak badly of the Justiciar or his bailiffs or of the Irish in anything whatever, and do not allow them to be disparaged in your hearing, no

130

matter what they say or do, lest perhaps they be incensed against you or yours on this account; but armed always with patience and kindness, overcome evil with good.

---

1.   *Registrum*, No. LXXVI.

2.   This letter was written before September 29 but after the visitation of Suir which Abbot Stephen carried out from the 27th to the 29th of August; the visitation was described in a report drawn up at Stanley after Abbot Stephen had departed from Ireland, and he indicated that he had appointed a monk of Furness as abbot of Suir during his visitation: see Letter 88.

3.   29 September.

4.   Connacht is the central-western province of Ireland, and included the monasteries of Boyle and Knockmoy; Connacht was the only province of Ireland still untouched by Anglo-Norman conquest and settlement, but in 1227 it was granted to Richard de Burgh; after he was appointed Justiciar in February 1228, de Burgh set out to conquer the province; see Otway-Ruthven, p. 94.

67[1]

TO THE ARCHBISHOP OF CASHEL,[2] greetings.
Coming to the house of Suir in response to the
obligations of the office enjoined on us according to the rules
of the Order and humbly exercising the terms of the mandate
we received, we found that startling conspiracies and plots of
rebellion quite unheard of for ages were wickedly prepared
like some sort of battle line drawn up against God and
the Order.[3]

Words would scarcely suffice to express nor a pen to
write down this series of events. Consequently, we refrain for
the moment from describing by letter such malicious temerity and perverse wickedness, but Your Venerable Paternity
can be informed of these matters in part by the bearer of this
letter. We have told him many things to be reported humbly
to Your Holiness; be so good as to trust him completely and
give him a favorable hearing.

Beloved Father, give your attention to this because the
aforesaid house of Suir is completely within your diocese and
jurisdiction, close to your city and cathedral seat.[4] Be
enkindled, therefore, with the zeal of the Lord and gird
yourself with Peter's sword,[5] with Phineas' dagger,[6] be a
shepherd by office, a father by affection, a monk by lifestyle,
and do not allow Dagon to set himself up against the religion
of God so close to the ark,[7] namely your cathedral church.
Rather, if it please you, let him be thrown down and
shattered with such fervor, eagerness, and deliberation that
the enemy may forever fear to dwell so close and to come
near the shadow of your wings.[8] Prostrate at the feet of
Your Holy Paternity, we ask this and exhort you with all
humility and devotion in Christ Jesus our Lord to endeavor
through your seneschals and bailiffs and through your

officials and deans to punish so severely an offense so great against God, the Church and the Order, for the sake of God and of your own honor, that the zeal you have for the Order will earn before God and men distinguished and deserved commendation for the effectiveness of your action, having fulfilled the office of a pastor as well as a monk of the Cistercian Order in the aforesaid matter with such great fervor and promptness and without any dissimulation or delay, that God and the Order and we ourselves and all our friends who are told of this will be placed under an obligation to Your Holy Benevolence in abundant thanksgiving; know for certain that we shall undertake with all diligence to report in full everything about the terms and proceedings of the aforesaid wickedness not only to the lord abbots of Cîteaux and Clairvaux but also to all our friends and to our representatives in the Curia and elsewhere, and we will be awaiting better times with the help of God, not forgetting that the Most High is a patient repayer.[9] Farewell.

---

1.   *Registrum,* No. LXXVII.
2.   Marianus O Briain, a former monk of Suir. See Letter 18.
3.   The events which occurred at Suir in the course of Abbot Stephen's visitation are later described in Letter 88.
4.   The monastery of Suir was situated about seventeen miles south-west of Cashel and within the archdiocese.
5.   Jn 18:10.
6.   Num 25:7.
7.   Cf. 1 K 5:2-5.
8.   Cf. Ps 17:8.
9.   Si 5:4.

68[1]

TO THE COMMUNITY OF STANLEY, greetings.
To report to Your Beloved the disturbances which we continuously sustain would be nothing other than to add affliction to the afflicted. Nevertheless, although a certain lay-brother of Dunbrody, our inseparable companion in all our journey through Ireland, was wounded with a lance almost to death,[2] still Divine Goodness by his grace has preserved us and our companions unharmed and safe and well so far, but we are in the deepest anguish not only because of the concerns of the Order committed to us but also because of the alterations made concerning you and our province. Therefore, we admonish you and we order you by virtue of obedience not to neglect out of any consideration for coin to pursue in all possible ways the concerns and liberties of our house and preserve the same intact, seeking the support of our bailiffs by gifts and by whichever other means you can and frequently approaching all our friends and those of our house, anxiously requesting them to be compassionate to our house and render assistance to you. For we are uncertain about our return, by which route or when we can make our journey, because the concerns of the Order involve us more deeply from day to day and the road through Wales has been closed to us by war. Consequently, we know nothing and can do no more, but we commend ourselves and yourselves, our house and our cause to God and to the glorious Virgin, and to the saintly patrons of our Order, Benedict and Bernard. Therefore, your holy way of life and vigil and devout prayers will seek to obtain from the Most High that which human effort cannot attain. Farewell.

1.   *Registrum,* No. LXXVIII.

2.   The reference is to the attack on the lay-brother whom Abbot Stephen sent ahead of him to announce the arrival of the visitor to the prior and community of Suir: Letter 88.

69[1]

TO THE BISHOP OF CHICHESTER,[2] greetings.
Wasted away with tribulations, burdened with dangers and sorrows beyond number so that we despair of life itself, we offer thanksgiving every day for Your Holy Paternity and we shall continue to do so as long as we live in all the ways we can in the sight of God and the angels because Your Distinguished Compassion, burdened in various ways with such difficult and important matters and so many unavoidable anxieties, was still willing to call to mind with gracious concern the preservation of the peace and indemnity of our house of Stanley, in this way bearing with us the burden of our tribulations and sending from far away some grace of benediction, some oil of refreshment, some honey-comb of consolation, lest perchance we be overwhelmed by excessive grief while affliction does not cease to be piled on affliction to the extent that, blessed God, wound does not leave place for wound. For, not to mention other things, some of our people at a short distance from us in the visitation of Suir were captured, thrown down, wounded, and beaten with sharpest scourges until almost their last gasp.[3] Each blow and each wound, God knows, transfixed our soul as well, in addition to the daily anxiety we have for all the monasteries of the Order in Ireland.

Further, certain evil men, God knows who they are, procured some robbers who stealthily pursued us every day from behind in so far as they could and dared; there were twenty on horse as well as those on foot, and every day they lay in ambush for our blood and that of our company. But by the grace of God we have already journeyed through all the Irish monasteries, creating new abbots everywhere from the other people and language, who certainly want to observe the proper form of religious life and to give attention to the peace of the realm, for they would not at all accept becoming harborers or dispatchers of robbers and murderers. We have so far escaped from the power of the same, and we are safe and sound in so far as the uncertainties of the times and harsh malice permit.

If therefore, Venerable Father, when we are surrounded by so many anxieties, pierced by the thorns of so many afflictions, we are also torn in our inmost being over our spiritual sons at Stanley whom we left sad and desolate on our departure, we believe that the weakness of our spirit, having been burdened with such an accumulation of labors and reasons for distress, will be unable to bear it. May we be allowed to speak our mind to our Lord and Father: we would prefer to retire and remain hidden during the brevity of these days which will be concluded shortly;[4] for there are anxieties everywhere for us and we do not know what we ought to do, seeing there the anxiety of our own sons in Christ, here giving our attention to the ruin of religious life in Ireland, for on the departure of the bearers of this letter, the monks of Maigue, hearing that we were preparing to set sail, joined together in an evil spirit of conspiracy; they violently expelled their abbot together with the English monks, and having brought in their own bullocks and cows and fortifying their church and dormitory, they presumed in their pride and frenzy to turn their monastery into a fortress.[5] This place is not more than seven leagues away from the city of Limerick,[6] and is situated completely in a land of peace which is far removed on all sides from forest or wasteland.

The prudent judgement of your well-tested discretion will know whether indeed it is becoming to the royal dignity or whether it is compatible with the honor of the Crown and the Church to endure such things. Indeed, throughout the whole lordship of Count Marshall,[7] or of Lords W. de Lacy[8] and Count H., his brother,[9] there is no one who resists or dares to make any move to rebel in any way at all against God and the commands of the Order. Whatever mishap and rebellion we have sustained has befallen us wholly in Munster where the lord King principally and solely holds the lordship.[10] But we pass over in silence the salvation of souls and the restoration of religious life, and the advantage, honor and peace which will accrue to the king and the kingdom as the results of our efforts through all those men who fear God and have the peace of the aforesaid country at heart, as well as in other ways of which the Council of the aforesaid Lord King can be fully instructed through the judges sent to that region. Therefore, lamenting the very shameful expulsion of our brothers and exposed to various dangers, we look forward day and night in tribulation of spirit to seeing the end of this, so that the wicked may restrain the audacity of their malice at least to some degree as long as they dread our presence. Consequently, prostrate at the feet of Your Holy Serenity and with as much insistence of affection as we can, we humbly supplicate that in respect of Jesus Christ and fraternal charity you deign to be the special defender of our cause with our Lord King until its conclusion. For Your Reverend Highness will keep in mind with what truth our cause is supported and with how many investigations and lengthy labors it has been carried out. What indeed we had remitted to the lord King for so small a concession in regard to the wood, so that in this way we would at least have a small portion assigned to us without the impediment of the foresters. What can be said of those people who, creating disagreement, strove to sow discord between the council of the Lord King and our house. Therefore, with an effusion of tears we pray to Truth who says: What to one of the least of mine etc.,[11] so that repaying Your Piety as you deserve at the Last Judgement, he will take up the defense of our cause and the enemy will not prevail against it. May Your Holy Paternity be well in the Lord for ever, and may the Most High preserve your well-being, and may it increase from day to day and accumulate glory and honor before God and men.

---

1.   *Registrum*, No. LXXIX.
2.   Ralph Nevill: *Handbook of British Chronology*, p. 216.
3.   This attack occurred on August 27 and was described at length in an official report drawn up by Abbot Stephen after he returned to Stanley: Letter 88.
4.   Jb 10:20.
5.   The rebellion referred to occurred in October, and was the subject of an official report drawn up by Abbot Stephen after he returned to Stanley: Letter 89.
6.   Maigue was about thirteen miles south of Limerick.
7.   William Marshall the younger, Lord of the Liberty of Leinster.
8.   Walter de Lacy, Lord of the Liberty of Meath, which included the monasteries of Mellifont, Bective, Shrule, Kilbeggan and Abbeylara.
9.   Hugh de Lacy, Lord of the Liberty of Ulster, which included the monasteries of Newry, Inch, Cumber, Grey Abbey and Macosquin. The lord of a Liberty was an hereditary royal agent to whom the profits of justice went, so long as he exercised his franchise in accordance with the law. The Liberties of Meath and Ulster were exempt and separate from the king's county of Munster and could not be entered by the king's officers. Only if the lord of the Liberty failed to execute a royal writ could the royal sheriff be specially authorized to enter the Liberty to execute it.
10.   The county of Munster, which comprised the counties of Limerick and Tipperary, had been permanently governed by a royal sheriff since 1210: see Otway-Ruthven, p. 82. Suir and Maigue, where the events Abbot Stephen referred to had taken place, were in the Lordship of Munster.
11.   Mt 25:40.

70 [1]

TO THE ABBOT OF BYLAND,[2] greetings.

We trust that, in your discretion, Your Holiness is aware that on account of the demands of our office imposed on us with the authority of the General Chapter it is necessary to send many monks and lay-brothers to monasteries of other realms, where they will receive the necessities with respect and will give themselves to the salvation of their souls by living ordinate. Consequently, we send the monk bearing this letter to Your Sincere Piety and we desire him to have commendation with you; we ask, we admonish, and by virtue of obedience which is owing to the Order and the General Chapter, we still more firmly enjoin you to receive the aforesaid monk kindly and to keep him in your house until such time as we discuss this matter with one another. Farewell.

---

1. *Registrum,* No. LXXX.
2. Byland (Bella Landa) in the diocese of York, England, a daughter-house of Furness: Janauschek, 104.

71¹

TO THE PRIOR AND COMMUNITY OF KILCOOLY, greetings.

We recall that with the authority of the Order and the General Chapter we had given a command to your abbot through the venerable abbot of Jerpoint and other devout monks of that house and through some of you, that, for the service of this house, especially in autumn, he should make provision to return to the house and be there when the visitation of his house was being made with the aforesaid authority. But by using evasions and finding excuses until now, he has contumaciously delayed returning, to the clear and serious detriment of his house; and we ought not to put up any longer with his negligence and his disobedience to the Order. Therefore, taking into account his inadequacy both by reason of infirmity, which keeps him almost continuously in the infirmary, and because he is lacking in the strength to rule the monastery and protect it against enemies, but especially because it is incumbent on us to absolve him from his office in that for the seven consecutive years that he was abbot he was never present at General Chapter, we depose him from the office of abbot with the authority of the General Chapter given to us in full power, absolving everyone of your house, monks and lay-brothers, from the profession they had made to the aforesaid abbot. In addition, with the same authority of God and the Order we fasten him with the chain of anathema unless he return the seal and the property of the house which he has, restoring them entirely to you. We subject to the same sentence all the persons of your house who accept the aforesaid man as abbot in future or obey him as if he were abbot. Take care of your house with all diligence and attention, in complete accordance with the counsel of your father-abbot of Jerpoint. We strictly prohibit the abbot of Jerpoint from appointing an abbot for you, however, for any reason except with the counsel and consent of the general visitors. Farewell.

1.　*Registrum,* No. LXXXI.

72 [1]

T O THE ABBOT OF BALTINGLASS, greetings.
We ask Your Prudence and we devoutly admonish
you, in the labor and burden which you have vigorously
sustained up until now for God and the Order, to strive to
persevere even to the end, never faint-hearted but always
strengthened in the Lord. [2]

Never, on any condition, receive T., formerly your
cellarer, who is a secret and deceitful conspirator, into your
house or its filiation. [3] We order you with the authority of
the Order to take the habit from him if he is found after the
period of time granted to him in the letter conveyed has
elapsed, because he was sent to the house of Fountains with
authority of the Order [4] but refused to go, fearing the sea
more than danger of soul and the evil of disobedience. Send
away the cantor of your house, not to return without the
permission of the General Chapter, because he himself wrote
the letter concerning the persecution of the abbot of
Baltinglass when he was in secret the perpetrator and the
principal promoter of the aforesaid conspiracy; and also
because while he was abbot of Abbeyleix he was very badly
spoken of on account of unchastity both at Kilkenny and
elsewhere to the scandal of the whole Order—this we ourselves have heard from men of authority who are very
worthy of trust—and further because those people who are
creating a wall of division in your house rely principally on
him, although in secret. Farewell. In witness of which
matter etc.

---

1. *Registrum,* No. LXXXII.
2. Cf. Is 35:4.
3. The rest of the filiation were the daughter-houses Abbeymahon and
Abbeyleix and the grand-daughter-house Kilcooly.
4. See Letter 54.

73[1]

T O THE BISHOP OF OSSORY, greetings.
We very much regret that we have to leave the region of Ireland without having personally taken leave of Your Benevolence. On which account, having received permission by letter, we do what we can at present and we offer abundant thanksgiving to Your Sincerity for all the honor freely bestowed on us and ours. We commend our daughter-house of Duiske to Your Reverence with all the devotion we are capable of. If it please you, may Your Holy Paternity effectively show whatever the humility of Your Devotion can do in regard to the same, and you may be assured that if you want anything from us that in any way concerns the advancement of you and yours we shall devoutly strive for it as if it were for ourselves. Farewell.

---

1.   *Registrum,* No. LXXXIII.

74[1]

TO THE ABBOT OF MAIGUE, greetings.

It seems to us amazing that you should order that all the wicked conspirators, the scandal of whom has already become known and will become known not only to the Order but even to the Church universal, be readmitted to their house this way, to the shame not only of that house but also of all the other houses of Ireland. For no-one would ever fear to offend the Order in future, but rather, with horns having been given to all the rebels here and elsewhere in perpetuity, this last error will be not just worse than the first[2] but the worst of all. Further, since we are preparing for our journey, we would not presume to grant dispensations of this kind for any reason without the knowledge of the General Chapter, for reasons any fool can understand. But since the visitation has already been commissioned, we advise you to indicate to the king of Thomond[3] and others that it is right to await other visitors, with whose advice, indeed, you should act with all prudence. However, we grant that you may receive only seven of those who are more easily led and less likely to cause harm, and introduce them into your monastery, suspended however from the performance of the sacerdotal and diaconal office until you receive the command of the General Chapter or of the general visitors. We do this out of respect for the king and queen of Thomond. When these other visitors come and the repentance of the aforesaid conspirators has been clearly established, however, they can show mercy to the same at the insistence of the aforesaid king and queen if they are convinced it is in accord with the advantage and honor of the Order; but any religious or secular who appeals to or supplicates with us for the above-named people in future will do so to no purpose until we have had the counsel of the General Chapter. Farewell.

1. *Registrum,* No. LXXXIV.
2. Mt 27:64.
3. Donnchad Cairbrech O Briain, king of north Munster or Thomond (Taudmumu); for the historical role of the king of Thomond see F.J. Byrne, *Irish King and High Kings* (London, 1973) pp. 165-201. Abbot Stephen expressed a poor opinion of this king in a letter written when he was Abbot of Savigny: *Registrum,* p. 112; Donnchad Cairbrech is described in a different light in his obituary in *The Annals of Inisfallen,* ed. S. Mac Airt (Dublin Institute for Advanced Studies, 1951) p. 353.

75[1]

T O LORD R. DE HIDA, greetings.
If it please you, take under your protection our
abbots of the other language recently appointed throughout
Leinster[2] for the honor of the lord count[3] and yourself and
for the peace of the land; should there be need, exercise your
power against rebels, monks and lay-brothers, by imprisoning
them and loading them with chains by the authority of the
Order and the General Chapter and ourselves, if the abbots
themselves request your help in this matter. Farewell.

---

1. *Registrum*, No. LXXXV.
2. French-speaking abbots had been recently appointed in Leinster to Jerpoint, Baltinglass, Abbeyleix, Monasterevin and St Mary's Abbey, Dublin.
3. William Marshall the younger, Lord of Leinster.

76[1]

To FELLOW ABBOT AND COMMUNITY OF DUISKE, greetings.

We order you by virtue of obedience within five days of receiving this letter to transfer all the abbots buried at Killenny up to your own house, and there discuss in your chapter as to where they can be suitably buried, each one in his own tomb. Do not receive Brothers Nehemiah and I . . . ,[2] your monks, sent out by you with our authority, into your house for any reason without the special permission of the father-abbot, because it is completely inexpedient for the peace and tranquillity of your house and even for its integrity. In witness of which matter etc.

---

1. *Registrum,* No. LXXXVI.
2. The name of the second monk is illegible in the manuscript.

77 [1]

TO ALL THE FAITHFUL OF CHRIST seeing or hearing the present writing, Brother S., styled Abbot of Stanley, greetings in the Lord.

It is fitting that one who was none other than a teacher of errors to those subjected to her be deservedly deprived of her authority as governess. The monastery of Maigue, stoney of heart and unyielding of neck, spurning the customs and salutary warnings of the Order, endeavored to administer the poison which it drew from the cup of Babylon[2] to all its filiation[3] while it was allowed to sit on a throne of pestilence and to spread the seed of pestiferous teaching with impunity. Although the General Chapter undertook in times past to apply cures of various types to so great an illness, the aforesaid house remains determined not only to bring no end to wickedness so that it might cease to engage in corruption, but has reached out its hand to wickedness, with its pride growing from day to day, forever adding sin to sin, not fearing to pile up new conspiracies on old. Consequently, if we who take the place of the General Chapter in fullness of power are very acutely urged on by zeal of religious life and by the reproaches of those who bring reproach[4] and if we impose harsher remedies in the aforesaid house of Maigue, and if following the example of Moses and Phineas[5] in hatred of evil and the destruction of scandal, we draw up the weapons of more rigid discipline, this is not absurd or at odds with reason, especially when goodness persuades, necessity impells, clear advantage and the salvation of souls determines [me].

Wherefore, with the careful and considered counsel of men of authority and of greatest experience, in order that the aforesaid house of Maigue may return more feebly to rebellion with horns polled and with wings clipped will not attempt the former flights of pride, by the authority of the General Chapter and the Order given to us in full power we subject the monasteries of Odorney[6] and Chore, formerly daughter-houses of the same Maigue, to the house of Margam as mother-house in future and we give possession of the daughter-house in perpetuity, decreeing with the same authority that whatever is claimed or attempted to the contrary at any time or in any way whatever is null and void. In witness of which matter etc.

The house of Furness has the same form of document concerning the monasteries of Fermoy[7] and Corcomroe[8] assigned to it.

---

1.   *Registrum,* No. LXXXVII.

2.   Cf. Jer 51:7.

3.   The rest of the filiation of Maigue were the daughter-houses Odorney and Chore and the grand-daughter-houses Corcomroe and Fermoy (daughter-houses of Suir). These houses were here allotted respectively to Margam and Furness. Suir had been previously allotted to Furness, and Holy Cross was allotted to Margam. Glanewydan had been suppressed.

4.   Cf. Ps 69:9.

5.   Cf. Num 31.

6.   Odorney (Abbey Dorney, Kyrie Eleison) in the.diocese of Ardfert, county Kerry, a daughter-house of Maigue: Gwynn and Hadcock, p. 123.

7.   Fermoy (Castrum Dei) in the diocese of Cloyne, county Cork, a daughter-house of Suir: Gwynn and Hadcock, p. 132.

8.   Corcomroe (Petra Fertilis) in the diocese of Kilfenora, county Clare, a daughter-house of Suir: Gwynn and Hadcock, p. 130.

78[1]

To all the faithful of Christ etc.

If novel and exceptional issues in our Order concerning the state of the houses of the Order bring about certain alterations and changes, this is not absurd or at odds with fairness, especially when goodness persuades, necessity impels, clear advantage and the salvation of souls determines. Therefore, inasmuch as lamentable charges made by God-fearing and religious men, with numerous accounts of the many disorders of the monasteries of Ireland, rise up to the hearing of the General Chapter and the word has spread even to the scandal of all religious life among both clerics and people everywhere, the aforesaid Chapter, desiring to apply a remedy to such a crisis and shame of the Order, and to meet, if it can in some way, such a danger to souls which is very earnestly deplored by everyone, decreed to send us with fullness of powers to all the monasteries of Ireland for the reformation of the Order there, so that together with other powers entrusted to us by the authority of the mentioned Chapter, we can freely assemble numerous monasteries into one unit without being obstructed by any opposition, even without seeking the consent of the father-abbots, and give them as daughter-houses in perpetuity to other monasteries of the same derivation for the reformation of the Order, and likewise impose interdicts upon opponents, suspend, excommunicate, regulate and administer everything in the light of what we consider to be advantageous.

As, therefore, placing the reward of obedience before our eyes and because of the requirement of the enjoined office, not without great and frequent mortal dangers going personally to the aforesaid houses of Ireland, together with other men of authority and discernment, both abbots and monks, and having reflected everywhere on the circumstances of the houses and of the persons living there and on the customs of the realm, we have been unable to arrive at any other solution by which the horrendous conspiracies and inveterate disorders could be brought to an end and religious life be restored, except that some monasteries, being taken away from subjection to disordered houses, be placed by perpetual law under monasteries of other lands as their mother-houses, who would be ready and willing effectively to restore the ruin of the Order both in spiritualities and in temporalities, so that each mother house has at least two daughter-houses in the before-mentioned land in order that whenever one of them attempts to shake its neck from beneath the yoke of the Rule with contumacious and malicious conspiracies against the Order or to foment schism, then the mother can at least find sanctuary and a safe retreat in the other daughter-house while she endeavors to curb the insolence of the other; in this way, on account of the differences of cases or times, she will more conveniently and advantageously remove the oppression and subdue the pride of the one through the other in accordance with what Ecclesiastes says: 'Better to be in partnership with another than alone; for they will have the advantage of the partnership. If one will fall, he will be supported by the other. Woe to the lonely, because when he shall fall he will have no-one to raise him. And if two sleep together, they will warm one another; but for the lonely, how will he find warmth?'[2] And so on in this manner.

Therefore, in the light of this principle and also many others of the same kind, and also having taken into account on the one hand the costs and dangers and on the other the many advantages and benefits to the Order, which if written down would exceed the proper and usual brevity of a charter with their excessive prolixity and would produce weariness in the hearers, and in addition having had lengthy deliberations with men of authority and of the greatest experience and having carefully gained the unanimous consent of them all, we subject the monastery of Holy Cross, formerly a daughter-house of Maigue, to the house of Margam as mother-house in future, and with the authority of the General Chapter committed to us with fullness of power we give possession in perpetuity as a daughter-house, that in this way an easier access and a freer path will be open to the house of Maigue as well as to that of Holy Cross for the quicker reformation and preservation in their proper state forever and every possible avenue will be shut which in the monasteries of Ireland has so far provided human audacity with the right situations and has given the necessary incentives for rebelling against the Order and causing detestable schisms in their pride and contempt. But, as it is to be feared that the outsider will freely admit himself and reap the fruits where anyone applies himself unwillingly and slowly to heavy tasks and to costly and especially dangerous labors, so with the authority of the above-mentioned Chapter we impose perpetual silence on all, abbots as well as monks and lay-brothers from wherever they may be, lest they be permitted to protest in any way against the aforesaid decree or to disturb it in whatever way they dare, and we decree that whatever is claimed or attempted to the contrary at any time or in any way whatever is null and void.

Therefore, the abbot and community of Margam are to strive in perpetuity to attend with such care and energy to the reformation in spiritualities and temporalities of their aforesaid daughter-houses that souls may be saved and lest on account of the clearly established transgressions and negligence of the aforesaid house of Margam in this regard, intolerable before God and men, may it never happen, the often-mentioned General Chapter be compelled sometime to change the mentioned affiliation.

In confirmation and witness of which matter we have placed our seal on the present writing together with the signatures of the venerable men who are witnesses of the above-stated matters: Lords J. of Margam, S. of Buildwas, A. of St Mary's Abbey, Dublin, W. of Maigue, . . . of Tintern Minor,[3] M. of Baltinglass, Ph. of Jerpoint, R. of Dunbrody, R. of Holy Cross, . . . [4] of Monasterevin, H. of Bective, T. of Duiske, the abbots.[5]

Given in the year of grace 1228.

1. *Registrum,* No. LXXXVIII.
2. Qo 4:9-11.
3. The initial of the abbot of Tintern Minor is illegible in the manuscript.
4. The initial of the abbot of Monasterevin is omitted in the manuscript.
5. Letters 77, 78 and 79 are the last official acts of Abbot Stephen's visitation and were drawn up at Tintern Minor very early in November; the abbots who witnessed this charter were there present with Abbot Stephen in a council to conclude the visitation; the notary omits to give the place of the meeting and does not include the names of the abbots of Tracton, Owney, Abbeylara, and Kilcooly.

79[1]

TO ALL THE FAITHFUL OF CHRIST etc.
   With wretched and incessant charges of the horrendous conspiracies and enormous disorders of Mellifont rising up on all sides to the scandal and shameful disgrace of our whole Order, the General Chapter of Cîteaux and the house of Clairvaux have been moved by maternal affection and have suffered greatly, not without reason, such infamy and danger of souls. For the aforesaid monastery of Mellifont, with a heart of stone and an untamed neck, spurning the customs and salutary warnings of the Order, endeavored to administer the poison which it drew from the cup of Babylon[2] to all its filiation while it was allowed to seat itself in the sides of the north and the throne of pestilence.[3] Wherefore, after having attempted remedies before this in many directions and in many ways, but in vain, the before-mentioned Chapter finally decided to send us to the region of Ireland with full powers in order to reform the Order; in addition to other powers entrusted to us by the General Chapter, it is permitted us freely to assemble numerous monasteries into one unit without being obstructed by any opposition, even without seeking the consent of the father-abbots, and give them as daughter-houses in perpetuity to other monasteries of the same derivation for the reformation of the Order, and likewise impose interdict upon churches and opponents, suspend, excommunicate, regulate and administer everything in the light of what we consider to be advantageous. Therefore, having given full consideration to the matter, we have decided it would be most beneficial and extremely necessary to assign the house of Mellifont, and also the monastery of Bective of the same area, in perpetuity to the house of Clairvaux as its rightful

daughter-house, having taken into account both its proximity of location and security and also the very many useful advantages which the house of Clairvaux will acquire in particular for reforming Mellifont and preserving it in its proper state in future. But because the aforesaid restoration will be very difficult and laborious and not the work of one day,[4] as we have proved with reliable information and with the witness of our eyes, by the unanimous counsel and agreement of men of authority and of the greatest experience, but especially of the abbots signing below, we have decided that the house of Bective should be strengthened and enlarged so that in future it can assist its mother Clairvaux in the aforesaid matter more conveniently and effectively. Wherefore, with the frequently-stated authority given to us in fullness of power we subject the small monastery of Shrule, formerly a daughter-house of Mellifont, to the aforesaid house of Bective as mother-house in future and we bestow possession as a daughter-house in perpetuity, decreeing that whatever is claimed or attempted to the contrary at any time or in any way whatever is null and void. In witness of which matter etc.

---

1.   *Registrum,* No. LXXXIX.
2.   Cf. Jer 51:7.
3.   Is 14:13 and Ps 1:1.
4.   Cf. Ezra 10:13.

80 [1]

1. The churches and chapels held by Master P. shall be conferred only on reliable residential chaplains in future, and not all on the one chaplain; rather, its own priest shall be in residence at each, apart from Ethelmolt which is of very minor importance.

2. All officials, monks as well as lay-brothers, shall render clear and thorough accounts to the abbot and the council of the house, and this shall be handed in in writing. If they conceal anything it will be held against the concealor for theft or the holding of property, and they shall sustain the penalties for it included in the Usages. It is forbidden under the same penalty for lay-brothers to sell anything without the consent of the abbot or cellarer.

3. Permission for going outside the boundaries for the purpose of conversation shall not be granted to monks because this is the breeding-ground of conspiracies and many disorders. Whoever transgresses in this or gives permission for it in future shall spend three days in light punishment, one of them on bread and water.

4. The law already in force in the statutes which begins thus: 'Since there is confusion concerning the use of meat', etc.,[3] shall be strictly observed under the penalty there laid down.

5. All blood-relatives of monks and lay brothers shall be completely removed from the monastery and the granges. Otherwise, the prior, the cellarer, the master of lay-brothers, and the lay-brother masters of the granges shall be on bread and water every Friday and shall be flogged in chapter as often as they transgress in this.

6. In order that the possessions of the house be not

uselessly squandered or the abominable crime of simony committed imprudently in future, it is strictly decreed under penalty of deposition in case of officials and discharge in case of members of council that monks shall not in future buy land or receive churches unless it is first established by means of a previous thorough enquiry that they can have clear right of entry and secure title.

7. Lay-brothers shall never eat or drink in the vicinity of the monastery or of the granges at the houses of seculars within two leagues except in the presence of the bishop or abbot. The transgressor of this very necessary decree shall spend three days on bread and water and shall be flogged that many times in the chapter of the monks.

8. Any monk or lay-brother, whenever he is intoxicated, shall be flogged in the chapter of the monks and shall be on bread and water.

9. No woman shall spend the night in the gate-house of the monastery because this is completely contrary to God and the rules of the Order. Otherwise the prior, the cellarer, and the porter, or the keeper of the Order[4] if the prior is absent, shall be flogged in chapter and shall be given light punishment for three days, one of them on bread and water.

10. No land shall be given in rent to any knight or man-at-arms in future.

11. No secular shall be served meat in a room or outside the boundaries, and no guest shall spend the night within the inner courtyard, except only Count Marshall[5] as a mark of respect; the horses of Master P. or of any others shall not be admitted for any reason into the monastery or the granges to stay; otherwise the prior and cellarer shall be subjected to the penalty written next.

12. At least two suitable seculars shall be deputed to guard the woods and cornstalks of the monastery lands, and no standing trees shall be cut down for burning while there is so much fallen timber. The lay-brothers whose servants have transgressed in this shall be sharply punished in chapter with very severe chastisement.

13. The house where the press was set up is to be divided from the courtyard of the sick with a solid, high fence, and both the rear of the servants quarters and the gate nearest the lay-brothers' infirmary shall be completely closed in by the feast of St Denis.[6]

14. No monk shall remain outside the monastery in the granges or at Killenny[7] for any reason; a secular chaplain specially appointed for that shall celebrate divine service there in future.

15. Junior monks within the seventh year of conversion shall profitably spend some hour each day in studying the Books of Usages and memorizing the church services.

16. For a period of two years no monk or lay-brother shall receive guests to stay in that house without our permission, and no-one sent out shall be transferred to any house of that region on account of its excessive poverty; they will be sent to monasteries of other regions where they shall be suitably provided for with necessities and shall be taught discipline.

17. The number of monks and lay-brothers is fixed; this number is by no means allowed to be exceeded without the special permission of the father-abbot; the number is thirty-six monks and fifty lay-brothers.

18. The monk who threatened to kill his abbot because he had not sent him to . . . *dines*[8] shall never be admitted in that house, nor shall Brother Gill; but they shall be provided for in monasteries of other regions unless they are forfeit.

19. In the strength of the Holy Spirit we strictly decree that everyone, monks as well as lay-brothers, shall bear themselves moderately this year and shall apply themselves in every way they can to helping and assisting this house so that it can rise up from the excessive burden of debts with which it is intolerably oppressed, lest, may it never happen, it becomes necessary to disperse the community next year.

20. Some final account of all the granges shall be audited in brief once in the year so that it may be known each returns to the monastery and what it receives, and whether their cost is greater than the produce.

21. No structure shall be built in future in the middle courtyard of the monastery or of the granges; it shall be built on the side within the confines on account of thieves and other chance dangers. Only solid roofing shall be constructed in any monastery in future.

22. No monastic allowances shall be given or sold to seculars in future without permission of the father-abbot.

23. In future lay-brothers shall not talk for any reason with monks in the refectory, dormitory, or infirmary in order that the regulations be observed.

24. The cross on the high altar shall be removed because the image is damaged, and candles shall not be placed in choir except on feast days when the sermon is given in chapter.

25. Monks and lay-brothers shall not ride for any reason to their relatives, kinsmen, or others, unless it is for the clear business of the house, something not ever to be arranged by the aforesaid monks or their kinsmen. Any officeholder who does otherwise or who gives permission for riding shall be deposed from his office without dispensation in the following visitation; if he has no office he shall take the lowest place of all for a month and shall be flogged in chapter every Wednesday and Friday during the same month and shall be on bread and water, because great necessity demands the setting of a severe punishment.

26. The general blood-letting shall be observed in future: completely according to the rules stated in the Usages. Otherwise, whoever then refuses blood-letting without clearly evident and reasonable excuse, to be given either to the prior or the keeper of the Order, or postpones it, shall not bleed himself at some other time of his own choosing.

27. The mass in the community on the days of the eves of festivals shall be said more slowly than is the custom and the psalms of the office for the dead shall be recited with a longer pause between half-verses.

28. It is strictly decreed that all exits and entrances between the outer and inner courtyard be completely closed up, apart from the large gate which is near the kitchen.

29. Neither the sub-cellarer nor any other monk shall on his own authority prepare or offer an extra dish, either in general or particular in the community, without the special permission of the abbot, prior, or keeper of the order. Whoever and however often he does otherwise shall be flogged that many times on the following day in chapter and shall be on bread and water.

30. The prior and sub-prior shall be watchful lest any monk or lay-brother expect a second meal without good, reasonable and necessary cause.

31. No charter shall be lent in future for any reason unless a proper record has been made of it and the special permission of the abbot himself has been obtained. Whoever transgresses in this shall take the lowest place for a month and shall be on bread and water every Friday and shall be flogged in chapter at the same time.

32. The carpenter shall be appointed to the grange of the castle by the Feast of All Saints.[9] Otherwise, the prior, cellarer and carpenter shall be on bread and water every Friday and shall be flogged in chapter for as long as this is neglected.

33. The cobblers-stall shall be completely transferred up to the same grange as soon as this can be conveniently done.

34. It is firmly decreed that no cowl be provided for any monk in future, either by gift or purchase, unless it be white.

35. The lay-brother who after our departure lifted up his heel[10] against the statutes of the Order and of the present visitation shall be sent out to another region, not to return except through the father-abbot, unless he worthily repents and refrains from such actions in future.

36. No structure shall be built in the granges, apart from a barn and shelter for animals, until the house is discharged from the burden of debts with which it is intolerably oppressed and until the monks' chapter-house and the guest-house kitchen are completed.

37. Because the unchastity of certain persons brings grave scandal on that house, it is firmly forbidden that

monks or lay-brothers who have been sent away on account of the aforesaid vice, or who shall be sent away for this reason, ever return except with the permission of the General Chapter as it is set down in the Usages.

38. In order that monks do not rush around through the town in a frivolous and immature manner, it is strictly decreed for the avoidance of the possibility of scandal that whoever is required to go to town on any matter shall go by horse.

39. All monks and lay-brothers who have possessions shall hand them all over to the abbot under penalty of excommunication and expulsion.

40. So that there will be uniformity in the Order, it is strictly decreed that in future the Rule shall be expounded only in French so that the less well-ordered do not conceal themselves and visitors when they come may understand and be understood by the monks. Whoever expounds it otherwise shall be subjected to the penalty allotted for breaking the silence for as often as he does so. No-one shall ever be received as a monk unless he knows how to confess his faults in French or Latin, regardless of whichever people he belongs to.

41. The Book of Usages and of New Provisions shall be read at supper for two years so that from now on no-one may excuse himself for not knowing them.

42. Whichever monk hears confessions, unless he is the confessor or has received the mandate of the abbot to do so, shall be sent away immediately lest he damage or damn the souls of his brothers in future.

43. No monk or lay-brother shall presume to interfere when the cellarers freely make distribution with the consent of the abbot of the corn and other things which they have in the granges, and lay-brothers shall not have a certain portion allotted them as if by custom. The lay-brother who interferes shall be sent out to another region. The same penalty is allotted to whoever sells any of the produce of the house without receiving the permission of the abbot or the cellarer in future. Whoever bestows anything, either animals

162

or money, from the property of the house into the possession or keeping of any secular at all without the permission of the abbot shall receive the same penalty.

44. Under penalty of the deposition of all officials and the discharge of members of the council, it is strictly forbidden that any woman ever in future be received as a nun on account of the greatest disorders and scandals arising throughout Ireland from such practices.[11]

45. On account of the complaint of Count Marshall and others, a suitable place shall be assigned to the nuns by the feast of St Michael[12] where they will construct their building and live in a more fitting manner in future. Otherwise, after this time for as long as they remain close to the monastery we place the whole monastery under interdict and suspend the persons there from divine services.

46. No monk or lay-brother shall interfere with or contradict the directions of the abbot so that he may freely administer through whatever persons he chooses and in whatever way he considers to be most advantageous for preserving the substance of the house both within and without. The transgressor of this precept was twice corrected and shall be sent away without dispensation if he needs to be corrected once more.

47. The abbot, the prior and other officials shall be more watchful and show greater care in investigating and properly restraining the unchastity of monks and lay-brothers so that the house does not suffer loss of good name in future. Other officials deposed from their offices shall be sent away and the abbot shall have to confess this fault in the General Chapter.

48. The Book of New Provisions shall be kept complete and amended; otherwise the prior, the sub-prior and the cantor shall be on bread and water for as long as this is neglected.

49. It is prohibited that lands or holdings of the monastery be alienated or even given to seculars to rent without the consent of the father-abbot. Otherwise, all officials who give advice or consent contrary to this shall be deposed without gainsaying, not to be promoted to any office within five years, and shall be sent out of the cloister,

not to return except through the father-abbot.

50. The sub-prior is exempted from being Master of Lay-brothers that he may better apply himself to watching over the discipline of the community.

51. The matter of the prior is placed in suspension while it is considered how he conducts himself in future in regard to the observances of the Order and paternal respect.

52. Monks shall not talk together except in the presence of the abbot, the prior, or the keeper of the Order.

53. The lay-brothers shall maintain the required silence. Otherwise they sustain the penalty for breaking the silence stated in the Usages.

54. No secular shall serve in the infirmary or enter the kitchens to prepare repasts of the community and infirmary. The prior and the cellarer shall sustain the penalty defined in the Usages as often as this occurs. The abbot shall confess this fault in the General Chapter as stated.

55. Sick monks as well as lay-brothers shall eat together in their own infirmaries, with the exception of the blind and bed-ridden.

56. The fixed number of monks for Mellifont is fifty, of lay-brothers fifty.

57. A very careful enquiry shall be conducted into which monks or lay-brothers are guilty through advice or consent or in any other way of that horrible deed which was abominably perpetrated against the abbot of Duiske and the prior of Dublin and their companions, and their names shall be told to us when we return or to the other visitors under penalty of excommunication.

58. Monks shall be more assiduous in the work they are accustomed to do and shall not carry out private works without proven necessity.

59. No-one shall be excused from sounding the gong unless he is exempted through the statute of the Order or by the abbot in chapter openly before everyone. The transgressors shall be denounced as severely censured and will be more seriously punished if there is the need.

60. A third part of the habits, hoods, cowls, and shoes

shall be given to the porter at the latest before the Feast of Blessed Martin[13] to be turned over for the use of the poor.

61. The infirmarian shall not speak with two monks together but only with one in the place set aside according to the rules of the Usages. Otherwise he sustains the penalty for breaking the silence.

62. The prior and the wardrobe keeper[14] shall make provision according to the rules of the Order for monks passing by as guests, so that a cowl, habit and socks are placed at the beds provided for them. Otherwise, both they and the lay-brother tailors shall be contented with only bread and the customary drink on the following day.

63. The infirmary of the poor shall be better provided for as decreed in the previous visitation. Otherwise the cellarer and the sub-cellarer, having been denounced for their obvious neglect, shall be flogged in chapter.

64. The three ring-leader lay-brothers who came from the grange to the monastery as fugitives and conspirators because they did not receive beer from the sub-cellarer on a certain fast day are to be subjected to the punishment for conspirators, although in their own house, until the following visitation. But we concede by the authority of the General Chapter that if the visitor is convinced of their repentance he can dispense them in part or release them completely.

65. The porter shall show himself more merciful and humane towards the poor.

66. The lay-brother cobbler shall have a monk with him who is informed of all the things which he does in selling, buying, giving, and lending. He will put these down in writing and will know how to make clear assessments of them.

67. Nothing is ever to be given, except by the porter and this from the alms-box assigned to the gate-house, to the fugitives who are making satisfaction at the gate-house to prove whether their humility is genuine, until such time as they are received.

68. To eliminate any cause for frivolity according to which expensive cloths of russet and other kinds used to be worn under the provision for grey cowls, to the shame of the

Order, and the monks frequently pestered the wardrobe keepers to have such cowls provided for themselves, it is very strictly decreed that no-one is to be provided with a cowl in future unless it is white. And if by chance anyone has received another as a gift or in some other way, it shall never be used in the community. As often as anyone transgresses in this he shall be flogged in chapter on the following day and shall be on bread and water on the same day.

69. Lay-brothers coming from the granges or living in the monastery who talk to one another in any way within the bounds of the monastery without permission, or who go outside the boundaries of the monastery only for the sake of such conversation, shall sustain the penalty for breaking the silence without any dispensation for as often as they offend in this way.

70. It is strictly decreed that in future there shall not be any different styles of painting, to look like marble or anything else, in the church or in other places of household-service; the simplicity of the Order shall be observed. Otherwise, the prior, the cellarer, the sacristan, and the keeper of work at the time of this disobedience shall fast every Friday on bread and water until the following visitation when they will be very severely punished.

71. Since the frequency of drinking produces serious disorders and dangers to souls, it is strictly forbidden for any monk or lay-brother to attempt to enter the refectory for the purpose of drinking between the community drinking time and supper in summer, or between lunch and vespers in winter, except just once or when they are with the abbot. Whoever goes against this shall be flogged in chapter and shall be on bread and water on the following day without dispensation and without regard to persons, except when on account of some solemn occasion the present punishment may be transferred to another day.

72. No monk or lay-brother shall dare to speak with a woman, he alone with her alone, either at the gate-house or elsewhere. The transgressor of this very important decree shall take the lowest place of all and shall be whipped once

166

each week in chapter until the following visitation.

73. No monk or lay-brother shall eat or drink within the confines of the monastery or within three leagues of granges, or receive hospitality in the homes of seculars, without the special permission of the abbot which is never to be granted generally to anyone. Whoever transgresses in this shall be on bread and water and flogged in chapter for three days.

74. Under the same penalty, irregular belts with elaborate stitching are forbidden to monks and lay-brothers.

75. The lay-brothers in the granges shall not attempt to drink outside the refectory on account of someone or other's presence, the only exception being their own abbot or another abbot of the Order. Whoever transgresses in this, as often as he does so, shall be content to have only water as a drink for forty days continuously.

76. It is decreed that the rules of the Order in chanting and psalmody shall be followed according to the writing of Blessed Bernard.[15] No one shall attempt to sing with duplicated tones against the simplicity of the Order. Otherwise anyone who transgresses in this, and the keepers of the chant unless they immediately restrain the aforesaid disobedient persons, shall be on bread and water on the day following and shall be flogged in chapter without dispensation for as often as he does so.

77. No one shall change his extra dish[16] unless it is on account of obvious infirmity, and fish shall on no occasion be served in the community for three days continuously and in place of vegetables, so that the rules of the Order are observed and illness of soul and body kept at a distance. There shall not be more than one extra dish for everyone at a single meal except at a time of visitation or blood-letting. Otherwise the prior, the sub-prior, the cellarer and the sub-cellarer shall be on bread and water for three days continuously and shall be flogged for a whole week in chapter, missing all extra dishes, for as often as they attempt to go against this.

78. The buildings outside the gate-house shall either come

down or shall be very carefully controlled and closed up by the Feast of All Saints, lest they offer an occasion for sinning or a suspicion of wrong doing. Otherwise the cellarer and the porter shall be on bread and water every Friday until the following visitation.

79. Precaution shall be taken for the time being that the cottage within the precincts of the monastery be closed according to the rules of the Order on account of the innumerable expenditures of the house and the serious danger of souls.

80. No delicate or very frivolous attire shall be provided for lay-brothers against the rules of the Order. Otherwise those who have them and those who provide them shall be on bread and water and be flogged in chapter every Friday until they give them up to the wardrobe keeper in the presence of the abbot or the master of lay-brothers.

81. Anyone found to be a malicious disturber of the peace or an evil abuser of the institutes of the Order shall be sent away immediately, never to return except with the permission of the visitors.

82. The cellarer shall provide enough lead to roof over the northerly part of the church.

83. The shrines on the window recess of the chapter-house shall be placed elsewhere according to the rules of the Usages.

84. All goblets from the mother-house shall be removed from the lay-brothers' refectory and they are never to have such a kind there. Whoever has them will be content with only water to drink for as long as he has them. It is forbidden under the same penalty for goblets worked with silver leaf to be provided in the monks' refectory. But, if they are cracked, they shall be mended properly with a strip of silver.

85. The lay-brothers shall not ask to be placed on a level with the monks when some favor is granted them in the refectory, especially on account of vigils or for illness, but they shall always partake of the general extra dishes according to the rules of the Usages. The lay-brother who disturbs any officials for the aforesaid reason by reproaching or com-

plaining shall not have an extra dish of any kind through a a whole week for as often as he does so.

86. No chapel or altar shall be built or maintained in the gate-house, and the structure already commenced shall be terminated as soon as it can be done with advantage. Otherwise the prior, the porter, and the sub-porter shall be on bread and water every Friday from the time of the unnecessary and useless labor until the following visitation and shall then be punished very severely.

87. The infirmary for the poor shall be suitably provided for with linens, and the sick shall be evidently better provided with suitable food and drink than has been the practice.

88. The lay-brother who eats in his habit without the hood outside the infirmary shall, as often as he does it, be flogged in chapter for three days and shall fast on bread and water for the same time.

89. No secular shall drink in the infirmary or shall be introduced into the refectory for the purpose of drinking unless in the presence of the abbot or by his special dispensation.

90. Goblets made wholly of silver or with silver bases, or spoons of the same material, shall not be used in the infirmary. No monk or lay-brother shall have a purse or knife except notaries and officials for the requirement of their office. Whoever has them shall be content with water to drink for as long as he has them until he has given them up.

91. It is strictly prohibited that secular boys or others eat in the infirmary kitchen. Otherwise the monk infirmarian and the infirmary lay-brother shall be on bread and water for as often as this is presumed.

92. The scriptorium in the cloister of the novices shall be removed and none other shall be constructed in future.

93. It is strictly decreed concerning monks traveling on horse-back that they keep the silence in accordance with the rules defined in the Usages. Otherwise they incur the written penalty for breaking the silence without any dispensation or regard to persons. The same is decreed for the lay-brothers living both in the monastery and the granges.

94. The porter shall not have a bed in the gate-house in future and he shall not sleep there; he shall observe the order defined in the Usages.

95. The master of the lay-brothers shall always go around all the granges within a five-week period to look into diligently the habits of the lay-brothers and correct transgressions.

96. Lay-brothers who have a monk assigned to their charges shall do nothing except with his knowledge; they shall arrange and dispose of whatever needs to be done by common counsel. The lay-brother cobbler shall not provide sandals for any monk, lay-brother, or other person without the permission of the abbot, the cellarer, or perhaps another monk whom the abbot has deputized for this.

97. The lay-brothers shall show more reverential respect than has been usual to monks, especially to the cellarers. Otherwise they shall be severely reprimanded and very sharply punished according to the manner of the offense.

---

1.   *Registrum*, No. CIV.
2.   This list was largely composed when Abbot Stephen was in the vicinity of Duiske and Jerpoint in August 1228; it begins the present sixth gathering of the manuscript, and was copied independently of the other fascicules, which follow a chronological order. This is the record kept by the visitor of the injunctions forwarded to each monastery he visited after the visitation had taken place. Some of the information would have come to his ears in the course of his private audience with each monk, which formed a central core of the visitation proper.
3.   *Statuta*, 2:4.
4.   The *custos ordinis* was charged with supervision in the cloister and dormitory.
5.   William Marshall the younger, Lord of Leinster. The monastery referred to is Duiske or another monastery in the lands of Earl Marshall.
6.   October 9.
7.   The monastery could be Jerpoint; Killenny had been a daughter-house of Jerpoint prior to its suppression as an independent house as a result of the visitation of 1227. It was united to Duiske, and the injunction could apply to Duiske if Killenny is here included in the category of granges.
8.   This word is partly erased in the manuscript; this is the ending.
9.   1 November.
10.   Cf. Ps 41:9; Jn 13:18.
11.   This injunction could not have been directed to Duiske or any other of the Anglo-Norman houses: it almost certainly refers to Jerpoint.
12.   29 September.
13.   11 November.
14.   The primary duty of the *vestiarius* was the clothing of the community and the provision of all necessary personal domestic effects.
15.   See the *Prologus in antiphonarium quod cistercienses canunt ecclesie*, ed. Leclercq, *SBOp* 3:515-16, and *Institutio Sancti Bernardi abbatis Claraevallis quomodo cantare et psallere debeamus*, ed. Chrysogonus Waddell, *Saint Bernard of Clairvaux*, CS 28 (1977) 187-8.

16.   This was the *pitancia* which, varying in number with the grade of the feast day, supplemented the 'general' dishes of the Rule. It also occurs above, number 29.

81 [1]

GREGORY, BISHOP, etc.[2] To the bishop of Salisbury. Having annulled, as justice would require, the election recently made of our beloved son W., Archdeacon of Winchester, in the church of Durham because it was carried out against the rules of the general council, and giving our careful attention because the more distinguished the same church is so much the more notable is its fall, we are compelled to give anxious consideration to the restoration of the same. For when there have been under the appearance of pastors wandering wastrels who not only took no care to correct errors or to gather together that which was dispersed but, not content with wool and milk, were even tearing the skins off the bones of the scattered sheep, the Lord's flock is lacerated and the church itself is gravely deformed in spiritualities and diminished in temporalities. Desiring for this reason to provide a suitable leader who, repairing the loss of former times, the Lord granting, will search for what is perishing, restore what is lost, and strengthen what is weak, we provide you to this church as pastor, expressing our hope that He who gives the virtues and requires the payment will restore this church to its former state and honor through the merit of your virtue, and further, will multiply pleasing increases in spiritualities and temporalities to the same church.

Therefore, since you ought humbly to accept that which has been carefully provided for by us, we ask Your Fraternity, we admonish and we urge you attentively through the apostolic writings in the strength of the Holy Spirit under the obligation of strict obedience, commanding and imploring you through the shedding of the blood of Jesus Christ, to put your shoulder to the task of carrying this burden which we impose on you, and with every evasion and excuse put aside, to go to the church without loss of time and administer it according to the grace given you by the Lord. Devote yourself to conforming to our will in this way and to obey our commands so that in avoiding the sin of disobedience you will show yourself to possess the blessing of willing obedience, and we will render you favors and kindnesses on account of this, knowing that if, which we do not believe, you want to indulge in laziness at this time and you refuse to accept the burden which encumbers us and we send to you imposing it, you should fear with good reason that we will require you to defend yourself in the last judgement before a severe judge. Given at Spoleto, 14 May, the second year of our Pontificate.[3]

---

1. *Registrum,* No. CV.
2. This bull of provision of Pope Gregory IX to Richard Poore and the next four letters (81-85) were copied into the Register around August 1228, at the end of what is now the sixth but should be the third gathering of the manuscript.
3. 1228.

82 [1]

GREGORY, BISHOP, etc. To our venerable brothers, the bishops of Bath[2] and Coventry,[3] and to our beloved son, the abbot of Stanley of the Cistercian Order of the diocese of Salisbury, greetings and apostolic blessing.

The mighty and merciful Lord wonderfully works wonders in his saints in heaven above and on earth below, and he adorns in their homeland those whom he has predestined to life and always glorifies some of them on the journey according to the magnitude of the riches of his wisdom and mercifulness for the edification of the faithful and for the strengthening of the catholic faith. We have been well informed by the letter of our brother R., Bishop of Salisbury,[4] and the chapter of Salisbury, that when Osmund of pious memory, Bishop of Salisbury,[5] received the church of Salisbury to rule at the very beginning of its foundation, he devoted great attention to the temporalities and greater still to the spiritualities. For he built the same church magnificently from its fundaments and he adorned it with books, treasures, and other things, including buildings and he enlarged its estates and possessions with lands of his own, and instituted prebends of canons in the same church with great deliberation, having gathered meritorious and praiseworthy persons there. In his time, too, God looked down from on high on this church and on the persons then established in it and bestowed such favor of his blessing on them that never in the whole kingdom of England did observance of discipline, integrity of customs, maturity of counsel, and weight of authority thrive in like manner; and the Lord so enriched Osmund in his works and so brought his labors to fulfilment that still for the greater part the English Church conforms itself to his ordinances; for he was

174

magnificent in piety and praiseworthy in holiness.

And in that he shone during his life with virtues and was resplendent after his death with the abundance of his miracles, the aforesaid bishop and chapter have pleaded with insistent devotion and devout insistence that he be included in the list of the saints, maintaining that it is proper for a treasure hidden for a long time to be revealed to the faithful and put like the lamp on the lamp-stand to edify many people. Because it is surely necessary in this matter to come to a decision with great care and prudence, we very strictly command you diligently, prudently, and carefully to carry out an investigation concerning the life and the miracles of the aforesaid bishop, and to arrange to have what you discover set down faithfully in writing and sent to us under your seals so that we may proceed as should be done in this matter. Given.[6]

---

1.   *Registrum*, No. CVI.
2.   Jocelin of Wells: *Handbook of British Chronology*, p. 205.
3.   Alexander Stavensby: *Handbook of British Chronology*, p. 233.
4.   Richard Poore.
5.   Osmund was the first bishop of Salisbury; he was consecrated bishop of Salisbury before 3 June 1078; he died 3-4 December 1099: *Handbook of British Chronology*, p. 251. He was canonized in 1456.
6.   The letter was issued by Pope Gregory IX from Assisi on 30 May 1228, and was received in England on 10 July 1228: *Registrum* p. 108, n. 1. This copy would have been delivered to Abbot Stephen at Duiske around August 1228.

83[1]

R., BY THE GRACE OF GOD BISHOP OF DURHAM,[2] to the venerable man and dearly-beloved friend in Christ, Brother S., Abbot of Stanley, greetings and a continuous increase of sincere love.[3]

Dearly beloved friend, all has happened as was pleasing to the Lord; all things are set under the power of his word and anyone who resists his ordering resists God. I was torn from my deepest being, as if I had been weaned from the breast of my mother[4] when it was said to me: 'Leave your country behind you and your household[5] and go to a place of horror and vast solitude.[6] Go to a defiant breed[7] and to a barbarous people, with whose language and customs you are not acquainted.' And the Lord knows that I would have preferred to leave the body or at least to live abased in the house of the Lord[8] rather than be tossed about like a leaf which is swept by the wind[9] the way I have been, and to be transferred in the same way from bishopric to bishopric,[10] if it were not for the fact that the cause of God was at stake and that the guilt for disobedience and the punishment due it frightened me; and I only wish to God that my spirit in which I am writing to you and my image might be conveyed to you, so that the calamity which hangs in the balance might become clear to you.[11] But blessed be God who has so softened so many of my adversities, distresses, and sorrows, and has in his kindness so tempered them that in part his consolations have gladdened my soul and in part he has restored me to myself. For behold, that which I always longed for, that which I strove for beyond gold and precious stones[12] has come about, for the Lord has exalted his saint, I mean St Osmund, and what had appeared difficult and almost impossible to obtain was through his merits achieved very easily and

176

readily and as petitioned in the Roman Curia, something which cannot be attributed to human industry or diligence. The authority of the supreme Pontiff has chosen the lord bishop of Coventry and yourself to conduct the investigation into the merits and miracles of the same saint. This is arranged to take place at Salisbury on the Monday immediately after the octave of St Michael[13] so that this very holy matter will be brought to the desired conclusion through your colleagues and yourself. Therefore, I ask Your Grace, and I entreat as much as I dare, that you be present on the aforesaid day and place, having put aside any excuse or delay; for your absence, may it never happen, would be more of a hindrance than would be presence of the others be a help, for Your Grace is very fully informed in this matter and your zeal and prudence can greatly hasten and effectively push forward the investigation which is to be made. Fare well and for long in the Lord.

1.   *Registrum,* No. CVII.
2.   Richard Poore.
3.   The letter was written after 16 July 1228 and was received at Duiske around August 1228.
4.   Cf. Is 28:9.
5.   Cf. Gen 12:1.
6.   Dt 32:10.
7.   Ps 78:9.
8.   Ps 84:11.
9.   Jb 13:25.
10.   Richard Poore was consecrated Bishop of Chichester in 1215; he was transferred to Salisbury in 1222 and to Durham in 1228.
11.   Cf. Jb 6:2.
12.   Ps 119:127.
13.   9 October 1228. The feast falls on 29 September.

84 [1]

GREGORY, BISHOP etc. To the chapter of Salisbury, greetings and the apostolic blessing.

It is not something novel and exceptional if the Roman pontiff, whose daily burden is the continuous concern for all the churches, should occasionally order and dispose in those churches in the same way as he promotes them according to his good pleasure. Consequently, we have come to make reservation for a prebend for our bestowal if there is one vacant in your church at present, or otherwise the one which is first vacant, commanding through the apostolic letters that you do not attempt to dispose of anything of this sort. We declare it null and void if any claim is made against this. Know that by our letter we have enjoined on our beloved son Master John of Rome, canon of Exeter, that should you act contrary to this he ought to make an annulment with apostolic authority, restraining those who oppose this with the ecclesiastical censure without appeal. Given etc. at Anagni 7 August, in the first year of our Pontificate. [3]

---

1.   *Registrum,* No. CVIII.
2.   This letter and Letter 85 following, the letter of John of Rome, concern the collation of Robert of Lexington, probably the brother of Abbot Stephen, to a canonry at Salisbury. This copy seems to have been sent to Salisbury by John of Rome with his own letter of 20 December 1227. The collation was first annulled, but was then approved by Pope Gregory IX on 26 May 1228: *Registrum,* p. 110, n. 1, 2. News of this decision would have reached Abbot Stephen at Duiske around August 1228.
3.   1227.

85[1]

TO THE VENERABLE MEN AND FATHERS, Lords, R., by the grace of God, Bishop, and the chapter of Salisbury, J. of Rome, Canon of Exeter, [sends] greetings and a servant's earnest devotion.[2]

You can be fully informed from his letter sent to you on this matter of the manner in which the lord pope came to appoint me as administrator of the prebend of your church. Therefore, desiring to follow the apostolic command, I earnestly request and I carefully admonish you, ordering you with the authority I exercise, to take care humbly and effectively to implement the apostolic mandate made to you. I then reserve to the bestowal of the lord pope the prebend which G. de Lacy, who died recently, held in your church, declaring it to be null and void if you have made any decision on this matter which is contrary to the apostolic mandate, with proceedings taken against you notwithstanding in the way that I will consider to be advantageous. Given etc.

Greetings. And if the good work which the devoted sons of obedience, the Cistercian monks who are bearing this letter, have undertaken can readily gain your support, we moreover earnestly request Your Very Sincere Beloved, for the sake of God and our love, to give whatever counsel you can to them in the business for which they were sent in accordance with what you consider to be advantageous, rendering whatever assistance they would consider helpful for them. Farewell.

---

1. *Registrum,* No. CVIX.
2. Written from York on 20 December 1227; received at Salisbury after 28 December: *Registrum,* p. 110, n. 2.

86 [1]

To THE MOST HOLY FATHER and Lord Gregory, by
the grace of God Supreme Pontiff of the Holy Roman
Church, Brother G., styled Abbot of Cîteaux, and the whole
community of abbots of the General Chapter [write],
submitting to you and in all things wishing you prosperity.[2]

With charges made by clerics and [lay-] people of great
disorder and enormous crimes in our Order in Ireland rising
up to our hearing from all sides on many past occasions, we
have been not a little saddened and wounded with heavy
grief and have sent as visitors year by year to the region of
Ireland capable men who, having God before their eyes,
would make careful inquiry into the reported offenses and
would undertake their correction in accordance with the rules
of the Order. In truth, they did not succeed in fully carrying
out the charge of visitation on account of the disobedience
and rebelliousness of the aforesaid people, and they themselves reported back worse offenses than those which had
been previously reported to us. Consequently, lest malice or
favor be imputed to our undertaking, whether through incon-
siderate haste or for want of foresight, we considered that
visitors of different languages, from Ireland itself, Wales,
England, Flanders, France, Lombardy, and many from
Clairvaux should be sent at different times with greater
power, and in succession they found the Order devastated,
the temporalities squandered, repeated conspiracies, rebel-
lions and murder plots, in addition to the extremely serious
and wicked excesses noted in the other letter; they deposed
some of the abbots according to the rules of the Order; they
sent other monks away from their houses to other well-
ordered houses; they punished others in different ways
according to the rules of the Order and strove in so far as

they could to reform the Order, but without success.

Consequently, the last visitors sent with the full powers of the Order received counsel from almost all the abbots of the neighboring lands who swore under the virtue of obedience that they could discover no other solution by which a conclusion would be brought to the horrendous conspiracies, inveterate disorders, and impoverishment of the houses, and by which religious life would flourish again, except that some monasteries be removed from subjection to disordered houses and be placed by perpetual law under monasteries of the same filiation in other regions who would be ready and able to restore very quickly the ruin of the Order in spiritualities and temporalities; in addition, the very poor and small monasteries, completely insufficient in themselves, were to be united with other monasteries in accordance with the rules and with regard to the benefit of the Order. They did this, indeed, to two very poor houses, adhering to the ancient constitution and custom of the Order by which it was beneficially provided that no house should remain an abbey which in fairness could not include twelve monks and an abbot.

Consequently, in that through the kindness of the Holy See since the foundation of the Order we have had the privilege that the Roman church has always ratified whatever was defined or decreed by us among the monasteries and members of our Order, and has never once committed the concerns of the Order to any persons outside the Order, except now at the insistence of a savage people and of fugitives from the Order in a letter obtained by hiding the truth and by false statements, as we have pointed out more fully in another letter; with all the devotion we are capable of we beseech Your Holiness on bended knee that with the accustomed kindness of the Apostolic See you revoke the investigation which you have committed to the archbishop of Armagh[3] and the bishops of Dromore[4] and Cloyne[5] to be made into our Order in Ireland, revoking as void anything they have done before your letter arrives to them. During the course of our General Chapter we were even prepared to alter the

181

manner of procedure of our visitation in Ireland out of respect for you and the state of the Order, not because of letters falsely obtained, as we said, if in truth it should be altered in any way. But none of those who procured the aforesaid letter nor their lawful representative appeared before us, and the visitors showed clearly before us that they have proceeded lawfully and in accordance with order. In addition, for the purpose of prevailing over all the malice of fugitives, we have entrusted the visitation and the alteration, if it should be done according to order, to some of our fellow-abbots, cautious and prudent men whom we have caused to be sent, out of respect for you, to the region of Ireland.

1.   *Registrum,* No. I.
2.   This letter was written at Citeaux by Abbot Gualterius d'Ochies on behalf of the General Chapter in September 1228, and copied at Stanley after Abbot Stephen's return from Ireland in November 1228. It is at the beginning of what is now the first but should be the fourth gathering of the manuscript.
3.   Donatus O Fidabra, Bishop of Clogher, succeeded the Anglo-Norman Luke Netterville as Archbishop of Armagh in 1227. His election as Archbishop was confirmed by King Henry III on 20 September 1227 when the temporalities were restored: *Handbook of British Chronology,* p. 307. Archbishop Donatus left England for Rome soon after 10 October 1227 when the king agreed to the union of Clogher with Armagh: *Patent Rolls of the Reign of Henry III,* p. 166.
4.   Gerald was bishop of Dromore before 15 April 1227: *Handbook of British Chronology,* p. 316.
5.   Daniel was elected bishop of Cloyne after 31 August 1226: *Handbook of British Chronology,* p. 325.

87 [1]

TO THE MOST HOLY FATHER etc. as above. [2]

Although it is totally unlikely in itself and we ourselves would not want to legislate for the monasteries of Ireland in a manner different from the houses of other nations in our Order, still their unheard-of disorders on many occasions and a certain deeply ingrained badness beyond anything customary have compelled us to make certain regulations concerning the state of the same, and induce us for the same purpose, not without sorrow, to describe certain crimes, although not fully, in this letter to Your Holy Paternity. Of these things, we have been quite convinced by the evidence of the abbots and visitors of our Order, by the charges of clergy and people, and by letters which have come to us. For in the monasteries of Ireland our restraint and rule is scarcely observed in anything apart from the habit, for there is no due service in choir, or silence in the cloister, discipline in the chapter, community meals in the refectory or monastic quiet in the dormitory according to the rules of the Order, not even as it is kept by black monks; for they live as they like outside the walls in huts wretchedly built out of branches [3] and they give their attention to all sorts of feasting and drinking; they reside all together in threes and fours, each of them having a horse along with his own boy-servant. As they do not have adequate provisions even for a small part of the year because they have alienated their lands and squandered their possessions for the most part, they rush around through the towns . . . . [4]

---

1.   *Registrum,* No. II.
2.   This letter to Pope Gregory was written and copied at the same time and places as the preceding letter 86.
3.   These charges were taken from Abbot Stephen's letter to the abbot of

183

Citeaux and the General Chapter, written from Dublin at the end of June: Letter 21.

4.   The remainder of this letter and the beginning of the letter following are missing due to a gap in the manuscript at this point; the hiatus amounts to at least one leaf of the manuscript.

88 [1]

. . . which could not be acquired in town either by gift or purchase.[2] The aforesaid prior with some others approached the before-mentioned lay-brother and taxed him with insults and very menacing threats. Then [the prior] jumped over a little hedge and entered the house of nuns completely conjoined to the monastery of the brothers where he commanded some scoundrels hiding there to attack the aforesaid lay-brother and serving-boys, and beat them up as they knew how. Which was what they did; for they threw the lay-brother from his horse and flung him to the ground; with both hands they completely stripped him of his shoes, socks and all his clothes except for the lay-brother's little hood which he barely kept, and they struck and beat him with fists, knees, and clubs from all sides, we speak the truth, almost to the point of death. The most serious assault, we are ashamed to say, was that they pulled and twisted his genitals in such a way that living itself became burdensome to him. They severely beat-up one of the serving boys; the other one alone escaped and brought the news to the town with his shouting. Therefore, a great commotion was made; the aforesaid prior and his accomplices were terrified and allowed the serving-boy to depart, and they sent the lay-brother, scarcely stuck on a horse, back to the town. He immediately took to his bed and was in no condition either to walk or to ride. Consequently, the aforesaid abbots secured a small boat and caused him to be transported by water to a monastery twenty leagues away, convinced that he would never completely recover.

Therefore, having given consideration with other prudent men as to what could be done, the aforesaid visitor sent ahead obedient members of the Irish people to forewarn the aforesaid prior and community concerning the obedience of the Order and to recall them kindly to the humility of penitence, but without success. Therefore, the aforesaid monks and certain abbots with them returned from the monastery and went to join the visitor; they reported that the prior had thrown off his cowl and stood in his scapular, with a lance in one hand, a sword in the other, and the scabbard hung around his neck. All the monks and lay-brothers, apart from the old and the ill, were his accomplices and were armed in a similar manner. The aforesaid prior swore under oath that he would first stab with his lance any of the monks and lay-brothers who sided with the visitor, and he added that if the visitor came, he himself would take the direct revenge upon him for the corrections made in the other houses throughout Ireland by doing to him what had been done to the lay-brother.

Therefore, as the visitor prepared to go to the monastery, the other abbots restrained him against his will, saying that although they were prepared to face danger with him neither they nor their other companions were prepared at that time to die. Since a good number of nobles and others had gathered in the parish church to hear a sermon by the same visitor, which he had promised to give on the previous Saturday when they devoutly requested it, they were told that death lurked within the gates for the aforesaid visitor at the hands of the above-mentioned malevolent men. Rushing from all sides to the abbots who were already approaching the monastery, they threw themselves into the middle as mediators between the visitor and his companions and the battle-line of the prior which was drawn up in his own way. Finally, after expending great effort the prior was scarcely brought to agree that the visitor might speak with him on condition that, if he were not satisfied with what he had to say, he would be returned to his own battle-formation without impediment or delay. Therefore, the frequently-mentioned visitor then began to entreat him kindly and humbly, asking him to recall to mind that he was a Christian man, a priest and monk, and especially a member of the Cistercian Order, which ought to have so much purity and

186

humility. But in reply, choked with pride and abuse, he poured out threats and invectives until finally, after a torrent of this, he lost the support of his followers, who now fully supported the visitor.

And so the before-mentioned visitor was introduced into the monastery by a community humbly seeking mercy and absolved in the usual manner; then having first delivered a devout sermon to the nominated electors, he gathered them into the church, and with their unanimous consent, God knows, he appointed as abbot a suitable man, lettered and of good character, who was a monk of their mother-house.[3] He deposed the prior as in justice he was obliged to do; he remained there for three days and, to the glory and honor of God, restored the discipline of the house and the Order as far as possible. All prudent and God-fearing men completely agreed that no-one from the rebellious Irish houses, for whose sake the Order had toiled so hard and had exposed its own to so many mortal dangers for fifteen years and more, should be appointed abbot until a set period of time had passed, so that in this way their devotion and obedience towards the Order would be proven in time, and they would first learn to be disciples according to the rules of the Order before becoming abbots, just as Joseph was first a good and faithful servant and afterwards a lord.

In witness of the truth of all this, the undersigned abbots have placed their seals: the abbots of Mellifont, Bective, Grey Abbey, and Tracton, together with the visitor.[4]

---

1. *Registrum*, No. III.
2. This official report, drawn up at Stanley after Abbot Stephen's return to England, November–December 1228, describes the visitation of Suir which Abbot Stephen carried out from the 27th to the 29th of August; he referred to this visitation in letters written in Ireland before the visitation had taken place (Letters 61, 62, 63, 64), and after it was completed (Letters 67, 68).
3. Furness was the new mother-house of Suir by a decision the council of abbots called by Abbot Stephen to meet in Dublin on 25 June; see Letter 22. Abbot Stephen had previously requested the abbot of Furness to provide a suitable monk whom he would have elected abbot: Letter 15.
4. These four abbots either accompanied Abbot Stephen on his departure from Ireland or else met him at Stanley; the abbots of Mellifont and Grey Abbey were not present in November 1228 at the council at Tintern Minor which concluded the visitation: see Letter 78.

89 [1]

THE VISITATIONS OF IRELAND being duly carried out according to the rules of the Order with the authority of the General Chapter by Brother Stephen, Abbot of Stanley and his companions at great expense and in repeated danger, some monks and lay-brothers of Maigue heard that they were on the point of departure to their own country, and they planned an unheard-of conspiracy and attempted to carry out some horrible deeds.[2] For they violently expelled and completely drove away from the monastery their abbot and the monks and lay-brothers who had been sent there with the authority of the Order to teach the rule, which was completely reduced to nothing there, and to reform discipline. In addition, turning the monastery, the cloister as well as the church, into a fortress against God, they stored thirty head of cattle, slaughtered and salted down, under the dormitory; they strongly fortified the dormitories of the monks and lay-brothers with great stones, stakes, palings, and weapons according to the custom of their people. They stored large amounts of grain, hay, flour and other necessities in the church and they placed vessels and containers adequate to hold water in the cloister; in addition, they strongly fortified a shelter above the altar with provisions and weapons so that they could live in it as if it were their keep. Finally, they brought thirty head of cattle on the hoof into the cloister, grazing them on the grass there and on hay stored in the church.

In addition, and we say this with shame and horror, each one of the monks and lay-brothers equipped himself as best he could with weapons prepared especially for him, excepting the old monks and some of the more prudent who left the monastery lest they become involved in such crimes. They joined with themselves under arms about two-hundred house-servants and lay-abouts of the district, partly by money, partly by other means. Therefore, with crimes of such a kind and such a degree having been perpetrated against God, the Church, and the Order, the abbot and aforesaid monks monks tearfully and most urgently requested help from the visitor in the midst of such great danger and scandal, lest in the same way other houses and peoples, especially the very remote, perpetrate similar things. He received the counsel of prudent and God-fearing men and applied himself modestly, humbly, and devoutly, through letters and suitable persons, that is the abbot of Owney and the cantor of Duiske, to admonish the aforesaid monks once, a second time, a third, fourth, many times, to cease from their inchoate malice and not to persevere in so great a disgrace to God, the Church, and the Order.

Disrespectfully spurning everything as if it were worthless, they ejected them with very serious threats. Finally, after suffering many such rebuffs, the sentence of lesser excommunication and then of greater excommunication for such unheard-of, obdurate rebellion were gradually and successively brought against them, and at last they were threatened that, unless they withdrew themselves very deliberately and quickly from such a crime, the secular power would be invoked against them to seize and imprison them, in the way that the Church has been accustomed to act in such matters. But they considered everything—warnings, threats and condemnations—to be of no account, and they rang the bells and rashly presumed to celebrate a solemn mass; they stripped the cloths from all the altars in the northern section [of the church] and, we speak the truth, they piled up heaps of stones; in addition, they ate flesh-meat publicly with their followers and accomplices in the cloister and the lay-brothers' dormitory. Finally, the visitor, who was utterly astounded and also perplexed about what ought to be done in this kind of situation, on the mature counsel of worthy and prudent men wrote to the lord bishop of Limerick,[3] at that time in attendance on the lord archbishop of Cashel, asking him to bring the before-mentioned ex-communicates to a spirit of saner council, or otherwise, out of zeal for the Church and love of religious life, to seize them and bind them with chains until through contrition and penance induced by punishment they deserved to be freed by the decree of the Order.

The aforesaid bishop kindly consented to do this out of zeal for justice and the honor of the Church, and he sent warnings with all diligence in person and through men of religion, and also his own official and various secular persons of authority, but in vain. When, therefore, the bishop him-self and his company were barred by force of arms from entering the monastery and the aforesaid excommunicates were being heinously harangued to launch an attack on the members of the council who had entered the monastery, so that they scarcely escaped, after five warnings had been given, he called together an assembly of clergy and noble laity; all that was left now to do was to seize the aforesaid rebels following the customary procedure of the Church. Therefore, the before-mentioned bishop prohibited everyone on pain of excommunication from plundering the possessions of the house or killing or maiming anyone, and he decreed that the aforesaid rebels were to be seized and brought to him and the tower they had built in the western part of the church was to be pulled down. He then took a position with his clerics outside the monastery and awaited the outcome.

Therefore, a large number of people broke in, and others from the opposing side battled fiercely, striking with the above-mentioned weapons, and two of the evil accomplices perished in the course of battle and of their wickedness, as was reported by the bishop's official and many others. The aforesaid excommunicates were brought before the bishop, but they were not prepared to give their consent to the judgement of the Order on any condition and they were sent away as fugitives on the decision of the bishop. The oft-mentioned visitor was engaged at that time in a very far-distant region, and when he learnt what had happened he went in haste in three days to the aforesaid house with other abbots of the Order. Together with a dean of the district sent there on behalf of the bishop, they renewed the consecration of the church and demolished the altar on which the aforesaid excommunicates had celebrated mass. Finally, having recalled some of the monks and lay-brothers seeking mercy and absolution, and having brought back into the monastery the abbot with the monks not involved in the aforesaid crime, the aforesaid visitor remained for some time in the before-mentioned monastery. When the disturbance had been quelled and the observance of religious life had been commenced there to the honor of God and the Order, the often-mentioned visitor together with his companions set out on his journey to the region lying on this side of the sea,[4] and he committed representation of the General Chapter to the abbot of Owney so that he might absolve and reconcile to the Order the above-mentioned excommunicates, excepting the four ring-leaders whose reconciliation he reserved to the General Chapter or to the visitor acting on behalf of the same as a threat and caution in the future. In witness of which matter the abbots of Mellifont, Bective, Grey Abbey and Tracton, together with the abbot of Stanley, place their seals.[5]

---

1.   *Registrum,* No. IV.
2.   This rebellion at Maigue occurred in October and was referred to in letters written by Abbot Stephen from Ireland at the time: Letters 69, 74.
3.   Hubert de Burgh: *Handbook of British Chronology,* p. 330. Limerick was a bishopric of the province of Cashel or Munster, of which the archbishop of Cashel, Marianus O Briain, was the metropolitan.
4.   England.
5.   This official report, and the one preceding, were drawn up at Stanley around November to December 1228, after Abbot Stephen's return to England.

90 [1]

To the Abbot of Maigue, greetings.

As it would be prolix to include in this letter counsel in a matter which is so important and so needful of careful attention, we have transmitted the purport of all our counsel through the bearer of this letter, Monk J., and we order you manfully to prosecute the aforesaid matter with the greatest prudence of discretion up to a satisfactory conclusion, not sparing the payment of money or of anything else to the Lord Justiciar and others who can help in this matter, being generous, if need be, to the point that the land remains wholly bare; for it is better that the possessions of the house be copiously expended for the cause of God and the Order than they be consumed by schismatics and excommunicates for the cause of the devil to the perpetual shame of the Order; nor should you or any of yours show any faintheartedness because we firmly believe that everything shall redound to God and the Order for glory and honor. Therefore, arm yourselves courageously, cheerfully, and steadfastly with the arms of patience and the strength of God, keeping in mind that, beyond any doubt, to the predestined, everything, prosperity as well as adversity, works together for the good.[2]

---

1. *Registrum,* No. VII; *Registrum,* Nos. V, VI are fragments resulting from the loss of a leaf or leaves from the first gathering of the manuscript and are omitted here. This letter and the three following were written at Stanley after the conclusion of the visitation, probably in the spring of 1229.
2. Rm 8:28.

91[1]

AGAIN TO THE SAME,[2] greetings.

With the authority of God and the Order and the General Chapter and under penalty of interdict and excommunication, we prohibit any of those excommunicated monks and lay-brothers who departed in the presence of the bishop from ever being admitted to the house of Maigue or to the granges without the permission of General Chapter, and know for certain that we will show our aforesaid prohibition to the Chapter itself.[3] Farewell.

---

1. *Registrum*, No. VIII.
2. This letter was sent to the abbot of Maigue together with the preceding Letter 90.
3. The General Chapter of 1229.

92[1]

TO THE NOBLE KING OF THOMOND[2] and his illustrious queen, greetings.

We protest as strongly as we can to God and to you as special friends of the Order the injustices and the shame inflicted to the great God, the holy Church and the Order through Brother T., monk of Maigue, your nephew, but a degenerate, and some other four monk-associates of his in the house of Maigue. We have excommunicated all of them with the authority of God and the Order, and we denounce the excommunicates to you on account of their manifest conspiracies and detestable schisms. In addition, we ask you as friends of the Order, for the love of God and the salvation of your souls, to take the aforesaid Monk T. captive wherever he can be found as a schismatic . . . [3] and a rebel even to the royal mandate which we have on behalf of the Order in Ireland, and when captured subject him to imprisonment and bind him with chains until he is freed by the General Chapter, doing this much that you may receive esteem, thanks, praise, and honor before God and men and the whole Order for the worthy revenge of the injury done to God and the Order, and you may deserve on this account to be a participant in all the prayers offered within our Order.

---

1. *Registrum,* No. IX.
2. Donnchad Cairbrech O Briain.
3. The two or three words following in the manuscript are illegible.

93[1]

The abbots of Maigue and Owney and Brother Vincent, Cistercian monk, have come to us and have supplicated humbly, devoutly and with every prayerful insistence on behalf of you and your noble wife the queen that we receive into Maigue freely and without censure of religion the monks and lay-brothers of that monastery who rebelled in an astounding and unheard-of manner against God and the Order and the holy Church, making a fortress of the church in defiance of all the decrees and canons of the whole Church and the institutes of our Order. Since such a terrible and serious act has reached the hearing of all the inhabitants of Ireland and has even, as we understand, already caused concern to the king of England, and since in addition the news of it has already been spread abroad throughout the kingdom of England and of France, we point out to Your Nobility that we ought not and would not grant the petitions of yourself or of the before-stated persons acting on your behalf who have come to us, because, since the honor of a king loves equity,[3] if we were to implement your petition against the law of equity, we would be the cause of great insult and shame to your Excellency and, what is worse, to the divine majesty, and we would incur the grave disfavor of the whole Order and the General Chapter whom we represent in this regard.

Therefore, we devoutly beseech you and we helpfully trust that if you desire the honor and reformation of the monks of Ireland, you will not permit any disturbance at all to be directed to the house of Maigue, to any member of the Order, or to the monastery of Odorney, and you will not allow any harm to befall any other house, knowing for

195

certain that there is no way in which the monks of Ireland can be more harmed than if the aforesaid houses or persons are vexed in anything. Venerable Lord, we beseech you not to be deceived by the monks and lay-brothers sent away from Maigue, whom we have deservedly excommunicated as schismatics and apostates by the authority of God and the whole Order and of the General Chapter; we have heard they are saying that no-one can excommunicate them, but the outcome of the matter proves the contrary. For the honor and safety of soul of you and yours, you should patiently await the arrival of other visitors. But, for your sake and reverence, we kindly grant that they can deal more mercifully with them, providing they see that they honestly admit their crime and humbly confess with sincere repentance, without pride or threats. We point out to you in the truth of Jesus Christ that this is the more secure and helpful counsel for your honor and for their advantage, because not even out of fear for our own death or of that of anyone else or for the burning of monasteries, could we in such haste change the sentence for so heinous an act. And know without doubt that unless the abbot of Maigue and his people live in peace, we shall cause the monastery with all its possessions and appurtenances to be acquired by exchange with the lord king or with some other ruler in the coming summer.[4] Farewell.

---

1.   *Registrum,* No. X.
2.   This letter was sent to the king and queen of Thomond together with Letter 92, preceding.
3.   Ps 99:4.
4.   This sentence was written before 21 May 1229 when Abbot Stephen delegated his authority as visitor to the abbots of St Mary's Abbey, Dublin, and Duiske: Letter 97.

94[1]

TO THE ABBOT OF DUISKE, greetings.[2]
If it is pleasing to the Lord and he directs our
steps at will, we shall embark for your area around the feast
of the Holy Trinity.[3] For we hope that the lord-elect of
Dublin[4] will have returned from the Roman Curia by the
aforesaid date. In addition, we are detained by various and
difficult matters which still hold us back from the mentioned
purpose. In the meantime, then, encourage all the newly-
appointed abbots by exhorting and imploring and even by
obliging them on behalf of the Order and ourselves, here
by letter, there by word of mouth, carefully to watch over,
to consult and make provision for their houses that we can
conclude our visitations and corrections in peace and joy, in
so far as one can in evil days and among such rough and
unlearned people.

We have learnt, if the reports are correct, that a man called
Charles, in name a Cistercian monk though in reality an angel
of Satan, stirs up the inexperienced, arouses conspiracies,
seduces the crowds and leads them into error against the
rules of the Order and the obedience to General Chapter,
and is plotting to destroy in Ireland that which the Lord in
his great compassion has planted and raised up. Wherefore,
we require Your Holiness with a very strict injunction to
summon the aforesaid monk to you either by word or letter
and sternly admonish him with careful and considered words
to restrain himself in future from such evil acts in deeds,
gestures, and words, so much more preferring the emblems
of humility, obedience, observance of the Rule, and giving
a good example in that he has grown out of and flowed
from a purer source and a holier root, namely our mother
Citeaux, if only he had not withered away! But if after

he has been first suspended from divine services he still proves obdurate, may it never happen, then on our behalf by the authority of the General Chapter and the Order bind him with the chain of anathema for his rebellion; denounce him for this and order the abbots everywhere that, if the aforesaid monk, persevering in his contumacy, can be found anywhere, they are to take away his habit which he does not deserve, lest henceforth under the skin of a lamb a ravening wolf within devours and disperses the sheep[5] for whom the most devoted lamb Jesus Christ poured out his blood.

In addition, admonish the abbots, in accordance with the rules given to them by God and the admonition received repeatedly from us, to stand in all steadfastness providently and prudently for the house of the Lord and, united in everything, let brother strive to help brother with counsel and goodwill so that the plantation and construction of the Lord[6] may be as hard to tear up and cast down the more as it is everywhere carefully supported. By admonition and counseling enjoin on the minor visitors to your region on behalf of the father-abbots not to make any attempt to alter the ordination concerning the correction of the state of the houses in Ireland made with the authority of the General Chapter by our indeed unworthy ministry; rather, they are to direct their attention to the peace of the abbots and to the rules of the visitation made by us, never upsetting the recently appointed abbots who have not refused to bear so many dangers for Christ, nor are they to inflict wound upon wound or add affliction to affliction. Otherwise, let them know for certain that, just as is fitting, we will consider as void the changes they make and we will besides severely punish them as rebels in our zeal for God and the Order. Farewell.

---

1. *Registrum,* No. LXXXX.
2. From Stanley before 21 May 1229. This letter and all those following form what is now the fourth but should be the fifth gathering of the manuscript, which was copied at Stanley immediately prior to and following upon Abbot Stephen's election as Abbot of Savigny, up to the time of his departure for Savigny in July.

3. 10 June 1229.

4. Archbishop Luke, previously chaplain to King Henry III, was elected Archbishop of Dublin before 13 December 1228; the temporalities were restored 22 January 1229; *Handbook of British Chronology*, p. 336.

5. Mt 7:15.

6. Qo 2:4.

95¹

TO THE VENERABLE AND BELOVED IN CHRIST, all the abbots, priors, communities and other members of the Cistercian Order who are in Ireland, and also to all the faithful of Christ: Brother S., styled Abbot of Stanley, greetings in the Lord.²

We have received the mandate of the lord abbot of Cîteaux and the General Chapter and also of the lord abbot of Clairvaux in these words:

Brother G.,³ styled Abbot of Cîteaux, and the whole community of abbots of General Chapter, to the venerable and beloved in Christ, all the fellow-abbots, priors, sub-priors, and communities, and other members who are in Ireland, and also to all the faithful of Christ, greetings in the Lord. Let it be known to all of you by this present letter that we have committed full powers through all the houses of our Order in Ireland to the abbot of Clairvaux and to the person or persons whom he chooses to take up the task with him or to delegate in his place, so that without any obstruction by opposition through all the afore-said houses, they can visit the monasteries as often as they want, without having sought the consent of the father-abbots, to depose abbots, accept their resignation from office and appoint persons in their places, send away monks and lay-brothers and expel them, change people to whichever houses of our Order they decide to send them, join several monasteries into one unit, give them in perpetuity as daughter-houses to other monasteries of the same derivation for the reformation of the Order, transplant monasteries and reduce them to granges, place churches and opponents under interdict, suspend and ex-communicate, expel persons, even by means of the secular power if necessary, and manage and dispose of everything as they consider advantageous. Wherefore, we strictly command each and every one of you by virtue of obedience that in all things you always obey the same abbot or his representative or representatives as if it were ourselves until they return to their own land. In addition, we ask all the faithful of Christ to render assistance to the frequently-mentioned abbot and the person or persons whom he nominates to take up the task with him, or as his representatives, in such a way that our Order may flourish again in the aforesaid land through your labor and endeavor and may return to its proper state, knowing that by doing this you shall be participants in all the good works which are done in our Order.

Given in the year of grace 1228, in the time of the General Chapter.

---

1.   *Registrum,* No. LXXXXI.
2.   This letter and the two following were written at Stanley on 21 May 1229. They form a charter on which Abbot Stephen transcribed the charters of the abbots of Cîteaux and Clairvaux for the purpose of notifying the monasteries in Ireland of them, and added his own instructions.
3.   Gaulterius d'Ochies.

96[1]

AGAIN TO THE VENERABLE etc., Brother G., styled Abbot of Cîteaux, etc., greetings in the Lord.

We strictly command you by virtue of obedience to accede to the admonition and will of our venerable fellow-abbot of Stanley in Wiltshire, or his representative, either with him or without him, in the carrying-out of the matter of Ireland in accordance with what seems to him to be advantageous. And if he wants to send any of your monks or lay-brothers to the region of Ireland, to remain there either permanently or temporally, you are freely to submit to him or his representative, setting them under the authority of the same abbot. Given etc.

---

1. *Registrum,* No. LXXXXII.

97[1]

To the venerable and beloved in Christ, all etc., Brother R., styled Abbot of Clairvaux,[2] greetings in the Lord.

Let it be known to all of you etc. as in the preceding letter.[3]

We, therefore, since we are not in a position to come in person to your region this year on account of demanding and unavoidable matters, and especially on account of the General Chapter, to which we have arranged, the Lord directing, to be present, we commit our office in every fullness of power, as stated in the above-written letter of the lord abbot of Cîteaux and the lord abbot of Clairvaux and the General Chapter, to the venerable and God-fearing abbots of St Mary's Abbey, Dublin, and Duiske so that they cannot cancel, or change in any respect, whatever ordinances, consolidations, confirmations, and bestowals were made by us, not without mature counsel and deep consideration, in the past year; but they will apply themselves as energetic and devoted dispensers of the multiform grace of God to water whatever has been planted, to build on the foundation laid down in Christ, and to insert gold, silver and precious stones.[4] For both the lord abbot of Cîteaux and the General Chapter, and the lord abbot of Clairvaux and the community of that place, have confirmed our beforementioned ordinances by unanimous approval. In addition, they have imposed perpetual silence upon all, abbots, monks and lay-brothers, from wherever they come, lest they attempt to complain in any way against the above-stated ordinance or to interfere with the same in any way at all. They also decreed that whatever is claimed or attempted to the contrary at any time or in any way whatever is null and void as is stated in their legally-binding directives provided with their seals affixed. We send a copy of these to you under our seal, keeping the documents themselves with us on account of the many dangers of the roads. And so we strictly command each and every one of you by virtue of the obedience which is owing to the Order and the General Chapter to obey always and in everything the aforesaid abbots of St Mary's Abbey, Dublin, and Duiske, or either of them if the other cannot be present, or their representative or representatives, as if they were ourselves, until you receive a legally drawn-up mandate concerning another visitation from the General Chapter or the lord abbot of Clairvaux. In addition, we ask all the faithful of Christ etc. as above.

Given in the year of grace 1229 on the Monday before the Ascension.[5]

---

1. *Registrum,* No. LXXXXIII.
2. Radulphus de la Roche–Aimon.
3. The commission of visitation from Letter 95 was included in this letter. Letters 95—97 made up one charter.
4. Cf. 1 Cor 3:8, 12.
5. 21 May 1229; 1228 is written by mistake in the manuscript.

98[1]

O THE ABBOT OF ST MARY'S ABBEY, Dublin,[2] greetings.[3]

We are obliged to delegate the visitation of Ireland enjoined on us by the authority of the General Chapter, for as we are hindered by various and demanding matters and desire to be present at the aforesaid General Chapter, we are not in a position to come in person to your parts this year. Therefore, having taken all the circumstances into account, we have decided to delegate the aforesaid delegation to you and to the abbot of Duiske, because we consider you to be possessed of zeal for the religious life and to be tempered by the moderation of discernment, and to have been instructed by the actual practice and experience of the region over and above the extent and requirement of the aforesaid matter. Further, the General Chapter will not allow its powers to be delegated for any reason to any abbot in charge of an Irish monastery until such time as the Order there be more fully reformed and it be more apparent that the old practice of rebellion has ceased for the future; moreover, the freedom of correction and the means of punishment would be obstructed for the aforesaid abbots by the importunity and the still untamed presumptuous audacity and headstrong ferocity of the Irish monks over whom they preside.

It will still be essential that no alterations to the houses are made this year, especially in major things such as the joining together or bestowals of the same, excepting only visitations, corrections, protections, consolations in the Holy Spirit and making of constraints, even with the secular arm if necessary, with the imprisonment of persons savage, uncontrollable, and rebellious. Everything must be done with eager zeal of the Lord with reference to place and time and the demands of the task. We have decided for your defense and protection and as a safeguard of your peace, which we desire sincerely in Christ, to set down in a charter[4] marked with our seal a number of established articles, drawn up by our administration and with the authority of the General Chapter for the reformation of the Order in Ireland.

Further, you can commit visitations more dangerous to and distant from you to abbots who are closer, having first however called them to yourself and instructed them very fully and with all diligence in what things, and in what manner, and with how much discretion they are required to act. Attend especially to the reformation of the daughter-houses of Clairvaux, and to the taming of the pride of Mellifont and also of Baltinglass, because it is situated in a central area and there is [through it] a continuous traffic of persons of the Order, and also the monastery of Maigue, making special provision in every way you can for the peace and tranquility of the abbots of Mellifont and Bective, and of all other abbots who behave without the scandal of dishonesty and who strive vigorously to subdue and vigilantly to reform their jurisdictions. Do not for any reason attempt to recall to Baltinglass any of those sent away or expelled from the aforesaid house, and do not allow others to recall them, and make every effort you can whether through the severity of your administration of justice and through the assistance of the secular arm, if there be need, to see that it is well supplied, both internally and externally, because this would be of great advantage to the Order and because there is continuous traffic through there.

Because we have heard that certain members of Whitland are more concerned that the abbot of Tracton (a vigorous and religious man, whose peace ought not to be disturbed in anything) and the community there speak the Welsh language than that they do the will of God and the Order, we strictly command Your Discretion to make sure that what we have decreed in regard to this matter and have laid down with the authority of the Order is guarded inviolate in all ways; forbid the visitors from Whitland from coming there so that they have no opportunity to disturb either the aforesaid abbot and community, or the rules of the Order which are coming to birth therein and which are imposed with the authority of the General Chapter. But if they do go, revoke as void with the often-mentioned authority whatever they are so injudicious as to do; if it is necessary in this regard, those who have transgressed the previously-made careful provision should be very severely punished with sentence of interdict, excommunication, or other penalty provided by the regulations.

Examine very attentively the letter sent to the lord abbot of Duiske[5] concerning the sedition, to be checked and also rather severely punished, of a certain Cistercian monk, not in fact but in name (which we say with sorrow), who, if the reports are correct, is attempting to spread discord and to stir up slumbering schisms; and having suitably applied in advance the appropriate admonitions and other remedies for such great temerity as are provided for by the rules of the Order and required by our profession, then proceed discreetly with the authority given to you gradually and vigorously to inflict the usual punishments very severely.

Further, in respect of the houses of Boyle and Knockmoy in Connacht, daughter-houses of Clairvaux, if you cannot find an abbot to visit them you can carry out the visitations through priors or others, at least two of that tongue,[6] men who are discreet and truly obedient to the Order, together with the abbot of Shrule, or without him, if it is necessary and expedient, [men] who will correct and regulate with all diligence in the aforesaid houses and also report their condition to you. Summon the abbots of the aforesaid houses and discuss with them the mentioned correction, completely drawing up the charter and the articles on it for the purpose of correction, as is convenient, and having put them in the order which is usual to be followed in visitations. With the authority of the Order, hand these over to the abbots to be carried out with all reverence and devotion. Recently-appointed abbots may stay away from the General Chapter this year on account of their newness and the necessity of reforming the Order; this you should enjoin very firmly on them all on our behalf with the authority of the Order. But the abbot of Inch, who remained away from the Chapter last year, should by all means come, and also the abbot of the daughter-house of Holm Cultram[7] if it is his year, or else persons substituted in their place if they themselves do not want to go.

Also, out of great favor, we grant the dispensation that, with the counsel of the abbot of Maigue, you can deal rather more mercifully with the conspirators of the same house on condition that before they have entry to the monastery, they return all the charters of the aforesaid house which have been maliciously taken away: and then, having long and carefully considered the matter, impose heavy penances on them, to be lessened as they deserve with the passing of time and with worthy contrition through which they will be stimulated from now on to strive after the obedience of the Order and the salvation of souls and to embrace them more lovingly in future.

Also, you can provide Irishmen as abbots to the monasteries of Connacht,[8] and Corcomroe, Newry, and Shrule, if they are vacant and it is impossible to be done more conveniently otherwise, on condition that you acknowledge absolute reliance in the Lord concerning their humility and obedience towards God and the Order. Do not on any account attempt to do this for other monasteries. We leave the vacant abbacy of Kilcooly to your disposal and, after having had discussions and very careful deliberation with abbots and other prudent men concerning its state, decide whatever is most convenient, advantageous, and carefully considered for the Order and for its daughter-houses.

Further, the abbot of Duiske and you should meet together immediately after receiving this letter and give immediate attention to the matter entrusted to you, admonishing all the abbots concerning love and especially about the grace of chastity, about moderation in drinking and unanimity with one another, so that each one applies himself to carrying the burdens of the other and brother to assisting brother.[9] If any abbots give rise to very serious and intolerable scandal, especially on account of unchastity or drunkenness, may it never happen, they are to be very sharply reprimanded and, if necessary, deposed. But on account of their inexperience other minor things must be tolerated very patiently and smoothed down little by little with the passage of time, so that at first let things be as they may but in time useless people and disordered customs should be changed for the better. Moreover, you will strictly forbid the recently-appointed abbots from going overseas without reasonable cause and moreover without your permission, or curiously wandering about and scurrying hither and thither; instead they are to give their careful attention to improving and reforming their houses with the help of God, always putting before their eyes the pride of place of their labor and their reward. Farewell.

He sent a similar letter to the abbot of Duiske.

---

1.   *Registrum*, No. LXXXXIV.
2.   St Mary's Abbey, Dublin, in the diocese of Dublin, county Dublin, a daughter-house of Savigny: Gwynn and Hadcock, p. 130.
3.   21 May 1229, from Stanley.
4.   Letter 99.
5.   Letter 94.
6.   The Irish language.
7.   This was Grey Abbey (Iugum Dei) in the diocese of Down, county Down: Gwynn and Hadcock, p. 134.
8.   Boyle and Knockmoy.
9.   Gal 6:2.

99 [1]

RTICLES TO BE OBSERVED throughout the whole of Ireland.[2]

1. No one shall be received as a monk, no matter what his nation, unless he knows how to confess his faults in French or Latin, so that when the visitors and correctors of the Order come they may understand [the monks] and be understood by them.

2. The charters and legal documents of the houses shall be carefully gathered together in safe keeping under lock and key, so that opportunity for theft or fraud by wicked men may be avoided in this regard in future.

3. The Rule shall only be expounded in French and the chapter of the monks conducted in French or Latin in future, so that in this way those who want to be received in future may attend school in some place where they may learn some gentle manners.

4. In punishment for the conspiracies having arisen throughout the Irish houses generally, it is strictly forbidden for anyone of that language to be appointed abbot for a period of three years, so that their obedience to the Order may be fully tested and they may first learn to be students that in due time and place they may become more capable masters without danger to their souls and to the Order.

5. It is forbidden under threat of anathema for lands or tenancies to be alienated without the consent and confirmation of the father-abbot having been obtained beforehand. This is decreed under penalty of deposition of officials and discharge of council members.

6. Property shall not be leased beyond a term of seven years so that in this way there may be recent memory of the transaction. It is forbidden to execute a lease except with

210

mature counsel and careful deliberation and with appropriate precautions having been taken in public with due solemnity.

7. In order that the property of the house be not uselessly squandered or the crime of simony committed imprudently in future, it is strictly decreed under the penalties mentioned that in future monks shall not buy lands or accept the patronage of churches unless it has been established through a thorough inquiry carefully conducted beforehand that they can have clear right of entry and secure title.

8. It is strictly decreed for all officials in the monasteries and in the granges who are in charge of the possessions of the monasteries that they render a true and accurate account to the abbot and council of the house or to those whom the abbot specially appoints for this. Whatever they conceal is to be held against the concealer for theft or the holding of property and they are to sustain the penalties therefore defined in the Usages.

9. It is decreed under the same penalty that lay-brothers are not to sell anything without the consent or permission of the abbot or the cellarer.

10. Monks or lay-brothers who have been sent away are not to be recalled without the special permission of the lord abbot of Clairvaux, and this is not to be sought through false statements or suppression of truth. For dispensation or pardon obtained in such a manner is to be considered invalid in law.

11. Under threat of anathema and penalty of deposition of officials and discharge of members of the council, it is strictly forbidden for any woman ever to be received as a nun in the aforesaid houses of Ireland in future, on account of the shameful disorders and scandals arisen from such practices.

12. By authority of the Order and the General Chapter, the abbots of St Mary's Abbey, Dublin, and Duiske are strictly commanded by virtue of obedience to promulgate throughout all the houses of Ireland all the above-mentioned articles, copied down word for word on separate

leaves with their seals affixed.

13. Each house shall have its own copy of these for itself. The aforesaid abbots shall order this to be read once each month through the whole year under sure and serious sentence of law and it is to be kept very carefully.

---

1. *Registrum,* No. LXXXXV.
2. Injunctions drawn up when Abbot Stephen was in Ireland (Letter 80) were translated into this list of general regulations in May 1229, at Stanley.

IOO[1]

To the abbot of preuilly,[2] greetings.

Having examined the text of your letter, we have clearly understood that Brother R., formerly your sub-prior, is to be recognized as abbot in future, for since the *Te Deum laudamus* has been sung with him present and standing among the abbots and afterwards remaining with them for some time, he cannot be released from the office of abbot except by authorization of the father-abbot of that house to which he has been called. Therefore, since the house of Champagne[3] is subjected to no small loss in spiritualities and in temporalities through the absence of its pastor, we kindly ask Your Sincerity with all the strength of devotion of which we are capable and we urge you in the Lord, beseeching you in the strength of the Holy Spirit, not to permit the aforesaid house of Champagne to languish any longer or be exposed to ruin, may it never happen, through the absence of a desired pastor but instead hastily to send forth the aforesaid Lord R., Abbot of Champagne, to his own sheepfold. For Your Grace well knows that we cannot install another abbot there, even if we wanted to, unless he first retired in accordance with the rules of the Order, although we would certainly not, however, accept his resignation for any reason. Therefore, let Your Benevolence give attention, if it please you, to the distance of Preuilly from our parts, to the cost and efforts of the monks in going and returning, to the danger to the house from the absence of the pastor, to our own sorrow for the damage to the house; and do not allow the aforesaid house to decay in its interior life because of the delay of its superior, when we firmly believe that on his arrival, the Lord favoring, it will be plentifully restored with manifold blessings.

213

1.   *Registrum*, No. XCVI.
2.   Preuilly (Prulliacum) in the bishopric of Sens, France, a daughter-house of Cîteaux: Janauschek 5. This letter and the following letter indicate Stephen's assumption while still at Stanley of the responsibilities of Abbot of Savigny, following his election on 24 May 1229 and notification of his election on 4 July 1229: Letter 105.
3.   Champagne (Campania) in the diocese of Le Mans, France, a daughter-house of Savigny: Janauschek, 188.

IOI[1]

TO THE ABBOT OF CHAMPAGNE, greetings.
Those whom God has joined together in the unity of
spiritual bond, let no man put asunder.[2] Wherefore, we
humbly implore the sweetness of Your Grace with many
tears, and we admonish and beseech you through the sprinkling of the blood of Jesus Christ,[3] completely putting aside
delay or excuse, to go quickly to the house of Champagne,
to the administration of which you have been called, not
without the inspiration of the Holy Spirit. Let neither
discouragement nor poverty frighten you away, for we are
prepared faithfully to assist you as a dearly beloved son in
every way we can. Further, the house does not owe more
than is owed to it and is well-provided for in necessities for
twenty-four monks. Your Devotion will keep in mind that
nothing can be lacking to those who fear God and seek his
kingdom. Most Dearly Beloved Brother, the very great
distance between Preuilly and our region, the great expense,
the detriment to the house, the danger to souls, the effort of
people in going and coming, our sadness and concern, let all
this restrain you from further evasions from now on. All
these things can arouse to the full the affection of compassion in a humble and devout heart, which we believe you
have. But if the aforesaid house is harmed in spiritualities or
temporalities by the continued absence of a pastor, we
shall summon you to render an account before the judgement-
seat of the Great High Judge. He will certainly demand
the blood of his souls from your hands.[4] Farewell in
the Lord, knowing for certain that the aforesaid house
can have no other abbot at this time unless death, may
it never happen, or ordered resignation dissolves the spiritual
bond already contracted.

1. *Registrum*, No. XCVII.
2. Cf. Mt 19:6.
3. Cf. 1 P 1:2.
4. Cf. Gen 9:5.

102

TO THE ABBOT OF QUARR, greetings.[2]
Coming to the court of the lord King, to touch on this just briefly, we obtained permission with every expression of his favor for crossing over to Savigny and for appointing a new abbot at Stanley. Wherefore, since the prolonged absence of a pastor is everywhere considered dangerous, we ask Your Devoted Sincerity in Christ, and we strictly admonish you by virtue of obedience, having God and zeal for the Order and the advantage and defense of the house before your eyes, to apply yourself to appointing for the aforesaid house such a pastor who can go out and come in with honor before his people, and, endowed with grace of life-style and learning, will employ himself in preaching the Gospel and will be competent and knowledgeable in fulfilling his ministry. In the strength of Jesus Christ and through the sprinkling of his blood,[4] we firmly adjure Your Holiness not to install a useless or unlettered man there for any reason unless, may it never happen, he is unanimously demanded by the electors; rather, the man you place there should be as much more dignified and praiseworthy a person before God and men, as the ears of the lord king, the magnates, the bishops, and many others are pricked up to hear which and how venerable is the person who ought to succeed us, although unworthy, in this place and responsibility. For we desire with all spiritual affection to promote hereafter such men as abbots throughout our whole derivation as know how to present the Word of God to his flock and have at least some slight ability to set down the affairs of the house in writing when there is the need. Further, since it is our greatest desire in Christ that the spirit be aroused and that spiritual things be preferred everywhere in our daughter-

houses, we seek to be informed through your letter whether all customs have been observed in the Lord concerning the ordering of your house, according to what was discussed and promised between us, before we cross over the sea. Also, know for certain that we love your person and your honor with all the inmost depths of love and we will always do so. But we desire that those who are lax and carnal be everywhere kept in submission, as is fitting, while those who are ardent for and act with zeal on behalf of God and the Order be exalted for the honor of the same.

---

1.   *Registrum,* No. XCVIII.
2.   Quarr Abbey, on the Isle of Wight, diocese of Winchester, was a daughter-house of Savigny and the mother-house of Stanley.
3.   This letter, like the two preceding, were written after Abbot Stephen's election as Abbot of Savigny, but while he was still at Stanley.
4.   1 P 1:2.

103 [1]

T O THE COMMUNITY OF STANLEY, greetings.
We have sent letters to the lord our fellow abbot of
Quarr in these terms: To the venerable etc. Coming etc.
down to: when there is the need.[2]

We come, therefore, to forewarn and forearm you as
dearly beloved sons in Christ in regard to the above-stated
matter so that, not taking any account of fellowship,
friendship, or any advantage of the kind, but only of those
things which are of Jesus Christ and for the honor of the
Order, you may give your attention to the most sweet Lord
with prayers and merits day and night, striving to obtain, in
accordance with the above-written rules, that his compassion
console you and provide you suitably with a worthwhile and
satisfactory father and pastor, who will be deservedly praiseworthy before God and men for his life and his learning.
Dearly beloved sons, may it never happen that in your house
there is that horrible and abominable prophet, that is, that
there is an idol or a demon raised up where the authentic
seats of life and truth ought to be. But if it does so happen,
which we say with sorrow, we will strive in whatever way we
consider to be right and with all our strength for the speedy
casting out of such wicked folly. Farewell.

---

1. *Registrum*, No. XCIX.
2. All but the last three sentences of the preceding Letter 102 were included
in this letter.

104[1]

To the abbot and community of Margam, greetings.[2]

Although our humble self blushes as much to write to command Your Venerable Holiness as to be embraced in the bosom of Christ, the urgent necessity of the Order and the pressing demands of the matter however compels me unwillingly to act in an unfamiliar way. Wherefore, by the authority of the Order and the General Chapter and the lord abbot of Clairvaux, we strictly command you by virtue of obedience to send with all speed, through one of your abbot-sons who are staying with you or another safe and secure messenger, that is, a vigorous and discreet monk of your house, the legally valid letter of the visitation of Ireland, which we entrust with the mentioned authority of the Order to the venerable men, the abbots of St Mary's Abbey, Dublin, and Duiske, lest the business of the Order, may it never happen, suffer on account of negligence in this regard. For, as you know, so demanding a matter requires the greatest urgency; moreover, by giving attention with such kindly solicitude to the support and reformation of your daughter-houses with that devotion and diligence which is proper, you will be making provision that from those houses to which you have given birth in sorrow, as is proper, you will when they come to maturity receive happiness and joy in the Lord. Farewell.

---

1. *Registrum,* No. C.
2. From Stanley towards the end of May or in June 1229.

105[1]

To the lord bishop of Durham,[2] greetings. We would regard ourselves as happy if we could explain the sorrows and tribulations of our heart, and the consolation of so affectionate a father were given to us to restore us in some way. Fearing indeed that perhaps, our faults demanding it, the Lord might have transferred us to a distant region and an unknown people, we were settled in a state of perplexity and distress as we did not know what we ought to do. The community of Savigny and the abbot-sons of the family unanimously and solemnly, as we have heard, chose us although unworthy and inadequate to be their father and pastor, with the lord abbot of Clairvaux having given his approval to this. Moreover, they sent to us formal messengers, the abbot of Aulnay,[3] the prior of Villers-Canivet,[4] along with the prior of Savigny, in fullness of power of the Order. These continued to make nothing of this known to us, and they kept the purpose of their coming to themselves until they would have us present in a chapter of our Order where, all of a sudden, they could place the burden on us and could determine the matter according to the laws of our Order. Consequently, they summoned us through a brother abbot by virtue of obedience to be present at Stanley on the Wednesday immediately after the feast of the Apostles Peter and Paul,[5] excuse having been put aside, to hear there from them the purpose of their journey and labor. Wherefore, tearfully prostrate at the feet of Your Paternity, we humbly supplicate with all the devotion we are capable of that in a moment of such dire necessity, Venerable Father, your consolation and counsel may not be lacking. For he knows, to whom nothing lies secret, with what reverence and joyfulness of spirit we always receive every-

221

thing which comes from your mouth as none other than words of life and a divine response. And so, in regard to the above-mentioned, may Your Paternity not delay, in the light of our need, hastily to return your counsel through the bearer of this letter. Farewell.

1.   *Registrum*, No. CI.
2.   Richard Poore.
3.   In the diocese of Bayeux, France, a daughter-house of Savigny: Janauschek, 99.
4.   This is perhaps the Cistercian nunnery of Villers–Canivet in the diocese of Sees, France, subject to Savigny: *Registrum,* p. 97, n. 3.
5.   4 July 1229.

106[1]

T O ALL THE FAITHFUL OF CHRIST etc.
Whereas we cannot attend in person to deal with the
matters and concerns which we have in the English kingdom,
we have appointed the beloved in Christ, Lord R., Abbot of
Dieulacres, as our representative; whatever actions he takes on
these matters, having requested the counsel of our monks
living in England, by doing, writing or disposing in any other
way at all, is to be wholly acknowledged and ratified. And, if
necessary, we promise as regards himself that the matter is
concluded in his favor. Farewell.

Brother William, monk of Savigny, had two copies of the
same kind of letter.

---

1. *Registrum,* No. CII.

107[1]

CONCERNING THE ENQUIRY to be made into churches and chapels. Concerning the ordination of rectors, priests, and clerics serving in them, and concerning their manner of living, knowledge, and solicitude for the well-being of their subjects.

Concerning the preparation of the sacraments and manner of distribution.

Concerning the ornaments of the churches, that is to say whether the vestments are clean, neat, and not worn out, the books are properly kept and are sufficient, and the statues and crosses are sound and not damaged.

Concerning the preservation of the eucharist, chrism, and oils.

Concerning the structure of the choir and church.

Concerning the properties and buildings of the churches, and concerning their proprietors, and which are burdened with pensions, and in what and why and how.

---

1. *Registrum,* No. CIII.

APPENDIX

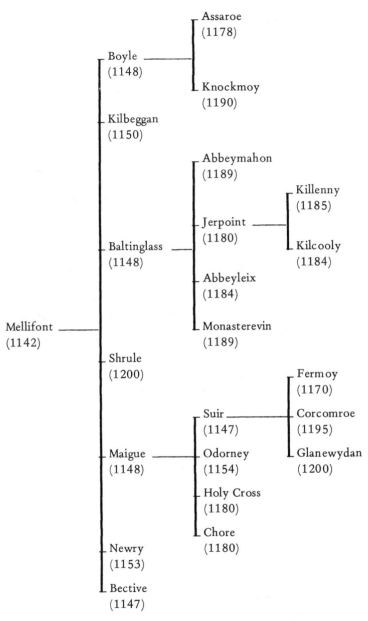

The dates of foundation are given in brackets.

THE CISTERCIAN MONASTERIES IN IRELAND

Macosquin

Assaroe

Cumber   Grey Abbe

Inch

Newry

Boyle

Mellifont

Abbeylara

Bective

Shrule

Knockmoy

St Mary's Abbey
Dublin

Killbeggan

Corcomroe

Monasterevin

Abbeyleix

Baltinglass

Owney   Kilcooly

Killenny

Holy Cross   Duiske

Odorney   Maigue   Suir   Jerpoint   Dunbrody

Tintern Minor

Fermoy   Glanewydan

Chore

Tracton

Abbeymahon

♦ CISTERCIAN MONASTERIES OF THE MELLIFONT FILIATION

❶ CISTERCIAN MONASTERIES OF OTHER FILIATIONS

◯ MONASTERIES SUPPRESSED IN 1227-8

THE ITINERARY OF ABBOT STEPHEN IN IRELAND IN 1228

▲ CISTERCIAN MONASTERIES OF THE MELLIFONT FILIATION

◐ CISTERCIAN MONASTERIES OF OTHER FILIATIONS

◯ MONASTERIES SUPPRESSED IN 1227-8

Macosquin

Assaroe

Grey Abbey

Cumber

Inch

Newry

Boyle

Melifont

Abbylara Bective

Mulingar

Knockmoy Shrule

Killbeggan

St Mary's Abbey
Dublin

Monasterevin

Corcomroe

Abbyleix

Baltinglass

Owney Kilcooly Kilkenny

Holy Cross

Killenny

Duiske

Jerpoint

Suir

Odorney Maigue

Clonmel Dunbrody

Tintern Minor

Fermoy Glanewydan

Chore

Tracton

Abbeymahon

→— JOURNEYS UNTIL REACHING DUBLIN IN AUGUST 1228

→»— JOURNEYS ON LEAVING DUBLIN IN AUGUST 1228

CISTERCIAN PUBLICATIONS INC.

TITLES LISTING

THE CISTERCIAN FATHERS SERIES

THE WORKS OF BERNARD OF CLAIRVAUX

Treatises I: Apologia to Abbot William, On Precept and Dispensation .... CF 1

On the Song of Songs I–IV . . CF 4, 7, 31, 40

The Life and Death of Saint Malachy the Irishman .... CF 10

Treatises II: The Steps of Humility, On Loving God .... CF 13

Magnificat: Homilies in Praise of the Blessed Virgin Mary [with Amadeus of Lausanne] .... CF 18

Treatises III: On Grace and Free Choice, In Praise of the New Knighthood CF 19

Sermons on Conversion: A Sermon to Clerics, Lenten Sermons on Psalm 91 .... CF 25

Five Books on Consideration: Advice to A Pope .... CF 37

THE WORKS OF WILLIAM OF SAINT THIERRY

On Contemplating God, Prayer, and Meditations .... CF 3

Exposition on the Song of Songs ... CF 6

The Enigma of Faith .... CF 9

The Golden Epistle .... CF 12

The Mirror of Faith .... CF 15

Exposition on the Epistle to the Romans .... CF 27

The Nature and Dignity of Love . . CF 30

THE WORKS OF AELRED OF RIEVAULX

Treatises I: On Jesus at the Age of Twelve, Rule for a Recluse, The Pastoral Prayer .... CF 2 *

Spiritual Friendship .... CF 5

The Mirror of Charity .... CF 17†

Dialogue on the Soul .... CF 22

THE WORKS OF GILBERT OF HOYLAND

Sermons on the Song of Songs I–III .... CF 14, 20, 26

Treatises, Sermons, and Epistles . . CF 34

OTHER EARLY CISTERCIAN WRITERS

The Letters of Adam of Perseigne, I . CF 21

Alan of Lille: The Art of Preaching . CF 23

John of Ford. Sermons on the Final Verses of the Song of Songs, I–IV .... CF 29, 39, 43, 44

Idung of Prüfening. Cistercians and Cluniacs: The Case for Cîteaux . . CF 33

The Way of Love .... CF 16

Guerric of Igny. Liturgical Sermons I–II .... CF 8, 32

Three Treatises on Man: A Cistercian Anthropology .... CF 24

Isaac of Stella. Sermons on the Christian Year, I .... CF 11

Stephen of Lexington. Letters from Ireland .... CF 28

THE CISTERCIAN STUDIES SERIES

MONASTIC TEXTS

Evagrius Ponticus. Praktikos and Chapters on Prayer .... CS 4

The Rule of the Master .... CS 6

The Lives of the Desert Fathers ... CS 34

Dorotheos of Gaza. Discourses and Sayings .... CS 33

Pachomian Koinona I–III:
The Lives .... CS 45
The Chronicles and Rules ..... CS 46
The Instructions, Letters and Other Writings of St Pachomius and His Disciples .... CS 47

* *Temporarily out of print*   † *Forthcoming*

Symeon the New Theologian. Theological and Practical Treatises and Three Theological Discourses... CS 41†

Guigo II the Carthusian. The Ladder of Monks and Twelve Meditations . CS48

The Monastic Rule of Iosif Volotsky .... CS 36

CHRISTIAN SPIRITUALITY

The Spirituality of Western Christendom .... CS 30

Russian Mystics (Sergius Bolshakoff) CS 26

In Quest of the Absolute: The Life and Works of Jules Monchanin (J. G. Weber) .... CS 51

The Name of Jesus (Irenée Hausherr) .... CS 44

Entirely for God: A Life of Cyprian Tansi (Elizabeth Isichei) .... CS 43

Abba: Guides to Wholeness and Holiness East and West .... CS 38

MONASTIC STUDIES

The Abbot in Monastic Tradition (Pierre Salmon) .... CS 14

Why Monks? (François Vandenbroucke) .... CS 17

Silence in the Rule of St Benedict (Ambrose Wathen) .... CS 22

One Yet Two: Monastic Tradition East and West .... CS 29

Community and Abbot in the Rule of St Benedict I (Adalbert de Vogüé) . CS 5/1

Consider Your Call: A Theology of the Monastic Life (Daniel Rees et al) . CS 20

Households of God (David Parry) . . CS 39

CISTERCIAN STUDIES

The Cistercian Spirit (M. Basil Pennington, ed.) ...... CS 3

The Eleventh-Century Background of Cîteaux (Bede K. Lackner) ...... CS 8

Contemplative Community .... CS 21

Cistercian Sign Language (Robert Barakat) .... CS 11

The Cistercians in Denmark (Brian P. McGuire) .... CS 35

Saint Bernard of Clairvaux: Essays Commemorating the Eighth Centenary of His Canonization. . CS 28

Bernard of Clairvaux: Studies Presented to Dom Jean Leclercq .... CS 23

Bernard of Clairvaux and the Cistercian Spirit (Jean Leclercq) .... CS 16

William of St Thierry: The Man and His Work (J. M. Déchanet) .... CS 10

Aelred of Rievaulx: A Study (Aelred Squire) .... CS 50

Christ the Way: The Christology of Guerric of Igny (John Morson) . . CS 25

The Golden Chain: The Theological Anthropology of Isaac of Stella (Bernard McGinn) .... CS 15

Studies in Cistercian Art and Architecture, I (Meredith Lillich, ed) . . CS 66

Studies in Medieval Cistercian History sub-series

Studies I .... CS 13

Studies II .... CS 24

Cistercian Ideals and Reality (Studies III) .... CS 60

Simplicity and Ordinariness (Studies IV) .... CS 61

The Chimera of His Age: Studies on St Bernard (Studies V) .... CS 63

Cistercians in the Late Middle Ages (Studies VI) .... CS 64

Noble Piety and Reformed Monasticism (Studies VII) .... CS 65

Benedictus: Studies in Honor of St Benedict of Nursia (Studies VIII) . CS 67

Heaven on Earth (Studies IX) .... CS 68†

THOMAS MERTON

The Climate of Monastic Prayer .... CS 1

Thomas Merton on St Bernard ..... CS 9

Thomas Merton's Shared Contemplation: A Protestant Perspective (Daniel J. Adams) .... CS 62

Solitude in the Writings of Thomas Merton (Richard Anthony Cashen)..... CS 40

The Message of Thomas Merton (Brother Patrick Hart, ed.) ..... CS 42

FAIRACRES PRESS, OXFORD

The Wisdom of the Desert Fathers

The Letters of St Antony the Great

The Letters of Ammonas, Successor of St Antony

A Study of Wisdom. Three Tracts by the author of The Cloud of Unknowing

The Power of the Name. The Jesus Prayer in Orthodox Spirituality (Kallistos Ware)

Solitude and Communion

Contemporary Monasticism

A Pilgrim's Book of Prayers (Gilbert Shaw)

Theology and Spirituality (Andrew Louth)

* Temporarily out of print   † Forthcoming